# RISING ABOVE STRIFE

## OVERCOMING STRESS

# RISING ABOVE STRIFE

## OVERCOMING STRESS

BY
NANCY INEZ WITTE

QUALITY PUBLICATIONS
P.O. BOX 1060
ABILENE, TEXAS 79604

ISBN O-89137-424-8

# RISING ABOVE STRIFE
## OVERCOMING STRESS

by
Nancy Inez Witte

THIS WORK IS DEDICATED TO BECKY.

To lovely Becky, a young Christian wife and mother of four lively, well-disciplined sons. After reading this manuscript, she had the inspiration to write—

Too often while reading or listening to a lesson, other people and their personalities come to mind; but never, or too seldom, do we consider ourselves.

I would like to see a book that begins—'This is FOR YOU, ABOUT YOU, and WITH LOVE TO HELP YOU''! We don't like to think of ourselves as talebearers, enviers, or causers of strife; but too many of us are and will not admit it, even to ourselves.

This lesson should come across to everyone who reads it. It did to me!

Becky Pounds

I wish to thank Becky for helping me find the courage to share this message with all our dear sisters-in-Christ; but I would have you know that the research which went into the writing of this book has helped me far more than it has helped others.

Nancy Inez Witte

Fill-in-the blank questions are taken from the King James Version of the Bible.

# Table of Contents

# Introduction

We are surrounded in these days of social upheaval by confusion and every evil work. The mature Christian woman will stay above it all. In union with the Lord she will not be entangled in the strife that exists between some individuals she knows and sees regularly; nor with strangers who might be inviting trouble.

Peace of mind, safety and comfort will be hers; not the absence of troubles, problems and worries, but the ability to cope with them. All this will be possible only by Christian maturity.

It takes time to grow to maturity. Development in the spiritual realm comes as naturally as in the physical; but only if healthy, growth-producing laws are observed consistently.

When one has become full-grown in the Christian life, she will have developed the ability to accept what cannot be changed. As goes the well-known saying by Reinhold Neibuhr, "Oh God, give us serenity to accept what cannot be changed, courage to change what should be changed, and wisdom to distinguish the one from the other."

Above the chaos of this world, the Christian woman has come to be a transformed person in thought, word and deed. This conversion has not been a hasty revision nor a sudden switch but an evergrowing awareness within herself and a diligent search for the change which she found only in Christ Jesus.

Was it easy? Yes and no. It was impossible in the days, months and years when she was trying to direct her own course; when she was asking God to answer her prayers according to the answers she had already devised in her struggles for self-dependency. Then, suddenly the load was lightened when she realized she could not determine her own direction, and cried to the Lord, "Oh God, I cannot help myself. Please show me the way." Is this possible? Absolutely! Once she has accepted without doubt the fundamental truth, "A man's heart deviseth his way; but the Lord directeth his steps" (Proverbs 16:9).

# AIM OF THIS STUDY

The intent of this study is to point out ways to overcome strife which are revealed in the scriptures whereby we can distinguish between the things that can be changed and the things that cannot be changed. Then, we want to learn to accept those things that cannot and have the courage, wisdom and understanding, in the Lord, to change those things which can be changed in order to contribute to our peace of mind and happiness.

This material is both positive and negative since we all have both positive and negative characteristics. It could be that we think we stand when we do not. We will be examining some of the characteristics and earmarks of things which lead to destruction. Our main emphasis will be on those things which lead to Christian maturity, salvation and peace of mind.

There will be some repetition in this study. But the repetition will be good because we will see the lessons in a new and brighter light each time.

Hopefully we will be able to examine ourselves throughout this study with honest intent and open eyes, and without embarrassment; making those changes which can be made and accepting those which cannot. Then this study will have achieved its purpose of leading us into more tranquil, peaceful ways of life and to an eternal life with God.

Then, there is the other side of the coin: that of helping those who may not realize the ungodly things that keep them and those around them in turmoil; and to lend them a strong, helping hand in getting on solid ground. It is very important that we recognize whether they can be changed or whether they cannot. It is also important to realize at what point we are being dragged down by them, and at such a time to save ourselves, knowing that not everyone wants to be changed and be saved.

Our biggest struggle is within our own selves, our own natures, since we are both physical and spiritual. The apostle Paul said, "For I delight in the law of God after the inward man; But I see another law in my members, warring against the law of my mind, and bringing me into captivity to the law of sin which is in my members. Oh wretched man that I am! Who shall deliver me from the body of this death? I thank God through Jesus Christ our Lord. So, then, with the mind I myself serve the law of God; but with the flesh the law of sin" (Romans 7:22-25). Paul also wrote: "For they that are after the flesh do mind the things of the flesh: but they that are after the Spirit the things of the Spirit. To be carnally minded is death, but TO BE SPIRITUALLY MINDED IS LIFE AND PEACE" (Romans 8:5-6).

Only by the grace of God and continual exercising of our own personal faith can we put the things brought out in the following chapters in their proper perspective. With constant faith and prayer God will lead us spiritually unharmed through all the difficult spots of life.

We will recognize the things that lead to stress-causing strife. Also, we will gain the wisdom and courage to avoid being led into strife. We will gain the strength and determination to make those changes within ourselves which are required to separate one's self from the wrong course.

So the aim of this book is to help you become more spiritually minded. It is my prayer that this book will lead you in such a way as to encourage discussion with Christian sisters, taking an honest look at the problem.

It is my prayer that readers will enjoy and grow spiritually by entering wholeheartedly into a class participation based upon this book.

Chapter One
# What Causes Stress?

The Lord favors one who loves peace and one who is a peacemaker; not one who continually strives or is the cause of stirring up strife. Continual strife does not have its beginning with any exterior motivation, but proceeds from the innermost heart of the instigator. "...those things which proceed out of the mouth come forth from the heart and they defile the man. For out of the heart proceed evil thoughts, murders, adulteries, fornications, thefts, false witness, blasphemies; these are the things which defile a man..." (Matthew 15:18-20).

So if we keep our hearts right with God he will direct our footsteps.

Have you ever found yourself in a quandary trying to escape the target position of the stress of another person's strife? This is a very trying position to be in! Do you have the concern and patience to stand before your mirror and take a good look at yourself and honestly evaluate the methods you have been using to deal with this person? Did you have the wisdom to determine if the relationship should be changed, or could be changed, or if it would be best to accept the situation and live with yourself peacefully as it is? Was your cause real or had you blown it all out of proportion in devising ways to put this person (or persons) in his proper place? When this did not accomplish its purpose, did you, with all good intent, switch to another well-planned tactic? Then another and another until in complete frustration "the game between you two" drew in other people and became a shameful, ridiculous spectacle? To you it became a seemingly never ending unhappy game.

Stop! Take an accurate evaluation of yourself, of the other party and of the situation. Spend much time in prayer, in study of God's word, in earnestly desiring to know the truth: Then, with a determined

1

dedication, follow the Lord and he will guide your deliverance from strife. For he has promised, "He that diligently seeketh good, procureth favor : but he that seeketh mischief, it shall come unto him" (Proverbs 11:27).

## THE STRESS OF EVERYDAY LIVING

We all live under stress—it is as unavoidable as activity and accomplishment. There are two kinds of stress. Success in whatever we do that is enjoyable or in being a winner is called "eustress" and is good for us. Failure is "distress" and is certainly bad for us.

The secret is to find the pleasant things we enjoy doing and which we do well and pursue them. Avoid the things for which we have no talent and so would fail to gain satisfaction in struggling with them. We learn pretty early in life to distinquish the difference. If we concentrate on our best talents we are going to be winners providied the stress we demand of ourselves is in proportion to our ability and desire to use our body and mind. This can be overdone and the stress becomes distress if we demand too much of ourselves.

We must consider our limits of time and energy when planning our schedules of work and our expectations of achievement. Remember the story of the tortoise and the hare? I am either fast or slow or in-between. If I struggle to time myself to all speeds I will be creating too much stress for both my body and mind. Then the thing I love to do becomes "distress" and harmful. What a shame to turn a work of joy into a burden of distress! Imagine the distress of forcing a tortoise to run at the speed of a hare; or of forcing a hare to slow his pace to that of a tortoise!

# For Private Meditation
# Or Class Discussion

INTRODUCTION

1. In the saying by Reinhold Neibuhr, what are the three God-given characteristics which are required in order to make the necessary changes?

    a. **Serenity to accept.** What are some things which we are compelled to accept after experiencing inner turmoil? Is it an easy thing to accept any of the following: the worldly ways of some people? disappointments? illness? injuries which are crippling? death? divorce? etc.?

    b. **Courage to change.**

        (1.) Myself first: What are the things *to be put out* of our lives named in Proverbs 4:24-27? If I lack the courage to change these things it is because I lack what? (Proverbs 3:5,6).

        (2.) Others and Situations: Why do we lack courage? What are some of the undesirable consequences of a lack of courage?

    c. **Wisdom to know one from the other.**

        (1.) Wisdom to know what can be changed and what cannot requires a knowledge of God's word. "Hear counsel and receive instruction, that thou mayest...." (Proverbs 19:20).

        (2.) Then we must understand what we have heard of God's word. Many people gather much knowledge about many things which they do not understand. These persons can never have wisdom, for "wisdom is before him that _____." (Proverbs 17:24a).

        (3.) Ecclesiastes 9:1 — "The righteous and _____ and _____ are in the hand of God."

        Wisdom is the exercising of what we have learned with understanding. With each use, we gain more knowledge and further understanding. Thus, we are able to know the things that can be changed from the

3

things which cannot. With the wisdom that comes from God we are able to live at peace with ourselves and with others; we can cope with life's inevitable problems tranquilly and with courage.

2. How does Proverbs 16:9 relate to the problem of strife?
   a. Does the Lord choose which way we will go?
   b. Then how does he help us in the way we choose?
3. If we fear to make changes, there are undesirable consequences, such as: living with a bad conscience, watching someone headed for destruction, not making use of our best potentials.
   Name others:

## AIM OF THIS BOOK

1. How can we distinguish between the things which can be changed and those which cannot? In other words, how do we determine whether it is best to accept things as they are or to try to change them?
2. According to the scriptures, where do we get wisdom? (James 1:5).
3. How does the dictionary define "wisdom"?
4. Wisdom is impossible without what? (Proverbs 4:7; 1 Chronicles 22:12).
5. Have you ever had a real part in helping someone change for the better and do you know the true joy that comes with it?
6. Have you led someone to Christ, or back to Christ? If so, what is the number one important thing you have done? (James 5:19-20; 1 Peter 4:8).
7. Have you ever decided that it is best to leave a situation alone? Why did you make this decision? Were you able to live serenely with it?
8. Have you ever tried to help a person and had to give up the attempt? How did you know when it was time to give up? We must endeavor to keep what? (Ephesians 4:3).
9. What kind of a mind is positively essential in order to help yourself or anyone else make changes for the better? (Romans 8:6).
10. "Above all these things put on _____ which is the bond of _____." (Colossians 3:14).
11. "Let the _____ rule in your hearts. (Colossians 3:15).

4

## FEARS AND WORRIES

Courage is the mastery of fear, not the absence of it. Our greatest lack of courage is due to fear. Fear brings on worries, distress and illnesses of all kinds.

Consider the following questions:

1. Do I fear failure before I begin and use this as an excuse to never begin?
2. Do I fear to take a stand for the Lord's way? Do I go the easy way and simply take no stand? Whose side am I really on if I take no stand? (Matthew 12:30).
3. Do I fear to use the talents I have? Why? What are the dangers of not using them? (Matthew 13:12).
4. Do I fear standing alone or being lonely? Do I have the courage to always extend the first hand of friendship?
5. Do I fear becoming ill or despondent? Despondency which continues more than a few days is a mental illness and is very prevalent in our society today.
6. How can we combat this kind of despair?

In times of illness, sorrow and trials, it takes special effort and awareness to remain steadfast. These times come to all of us sooner or later. A deep faith is the only thing that will keep us secure throughout life's pathway.

## QUESTIONS:

1. The causes of strife originate where? (Matthew 15:18).
2. Have you ever been in a situation such as described which developed into a "game of strife"?
3. Is your reaction when in a stressful situation to seek good or mischief? Can we expect to find what we diligently seek? (Proverbs 11:27).

## SELF EXAMINATION

Date of this examination:

1. I think my best personality characteristics are these: BE SPECIFIC.

    a.

    b.

    c.

2. In these areas I want to grow more pleasing to God and man: BE
   SPECIFIC.

   a.

   b.

   c.

Our trials help us to readjust our sense of values, to realize our
dependence on the Lord. Let us read and discuss Ecclesiastes 7:14.
"In the days of prosperity be joyful, in the days of adversity CON-
SIDER..."

3. Some things I should consider honestly about myself:
   a. Have I overreacted to situations too quickly and too nega-
      tively?
   b. Have I been stubbornly reluctant to yield to another per-
      son? Have I honestly considered whether the stand I took
      was honest or was it through selfishness, pride or self-pity?
   c. On first sight, do I judge whether or not I like a person? If
      so, how often have I been wrong in this self-deception?
   d. Do I consider whether or not I have brought this distressful
      situation upon myself?

Our thoughts are on the involvements of everyday living. Some of
them must be changed to protect both our spiritual and physical
health. Let us talk about some of our daily habitual patterns:
   1. Am I doing anything that really interests me?
   2. Am I doing too much, too fast, with too little satisfaction?
   3. Do I demand too much of myself and so am always tired
      and rushed?
   4. Do I have the courage to do some things that are more in
      tune with my talents so that I can feel successful? Example:
      Nehemiah 2:4-6.

Chapter Two
# Self-Deception —
# Another Cause of Strife

As the years roll by, the ways of mankind do not change. Jeremiah the prophet wrote these words about 600 B.C.: "The heart is deceitful above all things, and exceedingly corrupt: who can know it? I, the Lord, search the heart, I try the reins, even to give every man according to his ways, and according to the fruit of his doings" (Jeremiah 17:9-10).

God's people, as well as the heathen nations, were warned by the prophets of old of the pitfalls of self-deception. Before the Israelites were taken captive by the godless Chaldeans, Jeremiah continually warned them. "Thus saith the Lord: 'Deceive not yourselves saying, the Chaldeans shall surely depart from us; for they shall not depart' " (Jeremiah 37:9).

There are many ways in which we deceive ourselves. The most prevalent seem to be vanity and pride, self-pity, foolishness, and envy.

## VANITY AND PRIDE

God has claims upon those who are his children; so our obligations are not self-imposed but are of God. The things in this life which contribute to life's enrichment and to the glory of God are not in vain. All is in vain only for those who believe there is no God; those who live to glorify self rather than God. Thus, in vain do they seek after those things which promise no lasting reward. "For if a man thinketh himself to be something when he is nothing, he deceiveth himself...Be not deceived, God is not mocked: for whatsoever a man soweth that shall he also reap" (Galatians 6:3,7).

Even nations, through pride and vain disbelief in God, fall into chaos and enslavement. King David wrote many things concerning the great nation of Israel even in its prime, such as, "O ye sons of men, how long will ye turn my glory into shame? How long will ye love vanity and seek after falsehood?;" "The Lord knoweth the thoughts of man that they are vanity;" "God knoweth the secrets of the heart." To the heathen of his time David continued, "But Thou, O Lord, shalt laugh at them; Thou shalt have all the heathen in derision." "For the sins of their mouth and the words of their lips let them even be taken in their pride; and for cursing and lying which they speak" (Psalms 4:2; 94:11; 44:2lb; 59:8-12).

Obadiah the prophet said concerning the nation of Edom, "The pride of thine heart hath deceived thee—behold I have made thee small among the heathens: thou art greatly despised" (Obadiah 1:2-3).

At the beginning of the Christian age, the apostle John warned against deceiving ourselves through pride. He said, "We deceive ourselves, and the truth is not in us, if we say we have no sin" (1 John 1:8). Never a sinless man walked on this earth except Jesus Christ, the Son of God. His whole human existence was for this purpose. If we are cognizant of this fact and live to the best of our ability, under God's guidance we will know our weaknesses and dependency on the Lord. This will keep us humble. Surely Solomon was thinking of our generation when he penned these words, "There is a generation that are pure in their own eyes, and yet are not washed from their filthiness. There is a generation, O how lofty are their eyes and their eyelids are lifted up" (Proverbs 30:12,13).

It is frightening to compare our own beloved country with those things prophesied of nations thousands of years ago; which things came to pass according to both biblical and secular history.

SELF-PITY

Through feeling sorry for yourself you can become paranoid, devising wild imaginations that someone, or everyone, is out to deliberately hurt you. Feeling sorry for yourself begins with small things and can grow into a loathsome, never-ending habit. It is a self-centered vice.

The imagined and magnified feeling that no one likes me, no one appreciates anything I do for them, no one gives me credit for anything has ruled and ruined many lives from the beginning of mankind. It continues to ruin lives.

Self-pity is brought about by a feeling of inadequacy, born of self-concern and self-esteem. Just as Cain felt inadequate when his brother Abel's sacrifice to God was accepted and his was not. So, in anger and self-pity, Cain slew Abel. He then denied it and expressed no repentance. For these actions he was exiled for the remainder of his life (Genesis 4:16).

8

Even a congregation of the Lord's church can be guilty of wallowing in self-pity, but this is not always the case. There were fightings and fears in the Corinthian church. Paul was so concerned about its future stability that he wrote them a letter concerning a gross sin in their midst. They received it with godly sorrow, not with self-pity. In their godly sorrow they repented, approving themselves in their desire to be clean and pure (2 Corinthians 7:5-11).

FOOLISHNESS

The dictionary definition of a fool is: "a person lacking in understanding, judgment and common sense." The definition of "foolishness" is: "senselessness, weak-mindedness, heedlessness, thick-headedness and folly." In every walk of life we have foolishness to deal with. It certainly is one of the most noticeable of all self-deceivers of our times.

A portrait of a fool is drawn from the scriptures in the last part of this chapter.

ENVY—A MAIN CAUSE OF STRIFE

Cruden's Concordance defines "envy" as "discontent at the excellence or good fortune of another." There is not one good thing to be said about envy. Until we have learned to be content with what we have and who we are socially, envy will be a grievous detriment to our lives.

"Envy is the rottenness of the bone" (Proverbs 14:30). It is like a cancer that eats away one's spiritual innerparts. It cannot be satisfied at one victory but demands more and more because it is first of all motivated by selfishness. With a feeling of inferiority, an envious person tries to elevate himself by pulling another down.

We can all overcome envy if we are determined to do so. We must remember what it is and what it does. We must consider its companions and the strife it causes on this earth when at work. We must remember that it kills spiritually, that God will not tolerate it, and that all who are guilty of envy have set their own destiny.

To respect, admire and love the finer things in others as much as we do in ourselves is the key to staying free of envy. Remember that love "envieth not" (1 Corinthians 13:4) and that envy is to be laid aside as a dirty garment (1 Peter 2:1).

9

# For Private Meditation
# Or Class Discussion

## SELF-DECEPTION, VANITY AND PRIDE

1. What sort of a person would say he has no sin? (1 John 1:8).
2. What is Solomon's description of a person who is pure in his own eyes? (Proverbs 30:12-13).
3. The godless were taken in their pride by their speech. What three sins did they commit by their words? (Psalms 59:10-12).

   We speak of a person full of vanity as a "vain person." Webster's New Collegiate Dictionary defines "vanity" as "something that is vain, empty or of no real value, idle, worthless." "Having or showing undue or excessive pride in one's appearance or achievements, conceit." Solomon, the great philosopher, in his book Ecclesiastes, debates the values of this life. His conclusion is "_____" (Ecclesiastes 12:13). The vain things Solomon mentions are those things which are not enduring after this life. One paraphrase reads like this, "It is all useless, like chasing the wind." The King James version reads like this, "All is vanity and vexation of the spirit" (Ecclesiastes 1:1-2).

## COMPLETE THE FOLLOWING PROVERBS

1. "Everyone that is proud in heart is an ____." (Proverbs 16:5a).
2. "Pride goeth before _____ and a haughty spirit before _____." (Proverbs 16:18).
3. "When pride cometh, then cometh _____; but with the lowly is _____." (Proverbs 11:2).

## SELF-PITY

1. Too much self-concern and self-esteem make us victims of feeling inadequate. This leads to:
   a. Depreciating self because we measure success by someone we admire and try to copy, but fail. Name some things we often see in others and want for ourselves because of our human weaknesses:
   b. Wanting and striving for too much of this world and its goals. Name the three things this world (the worldly) desires the most: _____, _____,

10

_____ (1 John 2:16).
- c. How can we have enough confidence to face the problems of life? _____ (Ephesians 3:19).
- d. What should our attitude be toward those who have done a work that appears to be more important and more successful than ours? _____ (Romans 12:15a).
- e. What is love? (1 Corinthians 13:4,5). What does love do? (1 Corinthians 13:6,7).

FOOLISHNESS: A Composite Picture of a Fool
  Or One Who Exemplifies Foolishness:

What is the dictionary definition of "folly"?
1. (Psalms 53:1) What has the fool said in his heart?
2. (Proverbs 12:23b) "The heart of fools proclaimeth _____."
3. The words of a fool:
   - a. (Proverbs 18:7) "A fool's mouth is his _____, and his lips are the _____."
   - b. (Proverbs 15:14b) "The mouth of fools feedeth on ____."
   - c. (Proverbs 15:2b) "The mouth of fools _____."
   - d. (Proverbs 29:11a) "A fool _____."
   - e. (Proverbs 10:12b) "The lips of a fool will _____."
   - f. (Proverbs 10:13) "The beginning of the words of his mouth is _____, and the end of his talk is _____."
   - g. (Ecclesiastes 10:14a) "A fool also is full of _____."
4. (Proverbs 12:15a) "The way of a fool is _____."
5. (Proverbs 17:24) The basic lack of a fool is he has no _____ nor _____.
6. (Proverbs 17:16b) Why will a fool not get wisdom? He _____."
7. (Proverbs 10:21b) For lack of wisdom what happens to fools?
8. (Proverbs 17:12) It's better to meet what than a fool and his folly? _____.
9. Discuss Proverbs 17:28, "Even a fool, when he holdeth his peace, is counted wise: and he that shutteth his lips is esteemed a man of understanding."
10. Discuss the example of a fool in Jeremiah 17:10,11.


ENVY:

1. Let us examine some examples of envy in the scriptures and notice things which cause strife and every evil work.

11

a. Joseph's brothers envied him and did evil (Genesis 37:11).
b. Pilate knew that for envy the people delivered Jesus to be crucified (Matthew 27:18; Mark 15:10).
c. Miriam opposed Moses, giving an excuse. The real reason was envy of his authority and position (Numbers 12:1,2).
d. Leah and Rachel had a real problem with circumstances which were beyond their control. These two sisters, married to the same man, had only two alternatives. They could accept and learn to live peaceably in spite of their circumstances or they could be miserable and discontent, battling the unchangeable. They were not always wise enough to know the difference (Genesis 29:20-30; 30:14-15).

   Here are some ways that would have helped keep them from strife:
   (1.) Lean on a greater power than themselves.
   (2.) Know their problems, accept them serenely.
   (3.) Live happily one day at a time.
   (4.) Not let their minds dwell on what they lacked and what they could never have. (Philippians 4:1-8).
2. Let us notice what causes envy and with what it is associated:
   a. Why is envy one of the main causes of strife?
   b. To understand how sinful envy really is, let us note the other sins associated with it (Romans 1:29-32).
   c. There should not be envy in the Lord's church, but there is:
      (1.) Among members—
         (a.) Envious of one with more money, better home, car, clothing.
         (b.) Envious of one with more talents and achievements.
         (c.) Envious of one who has been assigned a special responsibility.
         (d.) Envious of one who is more popular, recognized and praised.
      (2.) Among preachers, elders and deacons—
         (a.) Envious of another who is more prominent than himself.
         (b.) Envious of other preachers, other elders, other deacons or even other members who are highly esteemed.
      (3.) Among congregations—

Because of a larger membership, faster growth, larger contribution, better buildings and other worldly things.

Chapter Three
# Distinguishing Characteristics
# Of Those Who Cause Strife

Someone is causing strife and trouble among us! Could that someone be me? I can know if I am a troublemaker, a fool, or a meddler by
a number of well-known marks of identity. Every individual has evi-
dent personality characteristics. It is essential to identify the source of
strife before we can begin to deal with it. This is not to say that all persons cause strife. Those who do will manifest some identifiable
characteristics. We will deal with a few of them:

A CONTENTIOUS PERSON

Contention seems to be more of a woman's characteristic than a
man's, but women certainly have no monopoly on this destructive
trait. Solomon advised, "It is better to dwell in the wilderness than
with an angry and contentious woman" for "a contentious woman
and a continual dropping in a very rainy day are alike" (Proverbs
21:19; 27:15).

Pride is the basic cause of all contention, for one full of selfishness
and pride is unreasonably conceited. In such a person there is no
wisdom. A contentious person is defined as "one likely to cause contention: one who exhibits a perverse and wearisome tendency to quar-
rels and disputes."

There are those who invariably turn every discussion into an argument; who seem to enjoy being forever picky and quarrelsome. Contentious persons seem determined to make their point of view accepted
by all (at least heard by all).

Even Paul and Barnabas had a contention between them which was
so sharp they parted and went different directions (Acts 15:36-40).

15

## AN ANGRY AND WRATHFUL PERSON

What more vivid picture could be put into words than these: "Surely the churning of milk bringeth forth butter, and the wringing of the nose bringeth forth blood; so the forcing of wrath bringeth forth strife" (Proverbs 30:33).

When a person does not control her anger she will invariably say or do foolish things. Guilt then takes over with all its frustrations because she had not controlled her tongue or guarded her actions. In vain are all the attempts which follow to cover up hasty words and foolish actions by other foolish words and actions. One gets more and more involved and draws other people into the strife.

There are two kinds of anger: a vexation to the ego which is to be avoided, and a vexation to the soul which is a righteous anger. Everyone gets angry at times. There are real and genuine reasons for anger. Jesus was angry several different times when he drove the profiteers out of the temple in Jerusalem at Passover time. No doubt he had watched these unholy temple fiascos with their various merchandising as far back in his childhood as he could remember, and, no doubt, with growing contempt for them. He was overcome with zeal for his Father's house (Mark 11:15-17). Can you picture the impact of his sudden display of righteous indignation as he poured out their money, overturned their tables and the seats of them that sold doves, and made a whip of small cords with which he drove the oxen and sheep out of the temple? There is a time for anger and a time to say something, and a time to take action.

During Jesus' display of zeal and righteous anger with those who profaned the house of his Father, he said very little. What he said was with authority, true, direct and to the point. He said, "Take these things hence. Make not my father's house a house of merchandise. It is written, 'My house shall be called the house of prayer,' but ye have made it a den of thieves" (Matthew 21:12,13; *cf.* Mark 11:15-17; Luke 19:45,46; John 2:14-16).

Although Jesus was angry he did not sin. He was "about his Father's business."

## A BUSYBODY AND MEDDLER

Paul wrote words of wisdom to Timothy about women who did not occupy their time at home as God intended they should. He wrote, "And withal they learn to be idle, but tattlers also and busybodies, speaking things which they ought not" (1 Timothy 5:13).

A thousand years before, Solomon had given this wise advice:

16

"Withdraw thy foot from thy neighbors house, lest he be weary of thee and so hate thee" (Proverbs 25:17).

Is it not sad to see a woman who has so little interest in her home, her husband and her children that time weighs heavily upon her hands? So, in simple boredom she daily seeks out a neighbor for morning coffee. When these "welcomes" are worn thin, she will take to the telephone to find someone available to go, go, go, at any time, with most anyone most anywhere. She will do anything from selfish self-pity to avoid boredom.

This type of a person puts our Christianity through a thorough testing. Great patience and compassion in dealing with her is a must. She desires to be with the seemingly popular women (whether in the church or out), those who are the most active and their time most occupied by doing good for other people. If her demands are not always honored she may imagine, in her self-pity, that she is not liked. Then she comes to the only conclusion she can, "How can I be friends with someone who does not like me?" Oh that she would only open her eyes and her mind and ask God for wisdom! For, "He that is void of wisdom despiseth his neighbor" (Proverbs 11:12a).

In the final analysis she will find herself only with those of her same way of life; only with those who waste precious time in telling and being told the latest newsy gossip, in meddling in the affairs of those who are doing good works, and/or in enjoying the company of those who are worldly—it will grow to make no difference to her.

Do a little testing for yourself! The next time you go to clean house for a sick friend, or need some cookies baked to take along, ask a busybody if she will come along to help and spend some valuable time with you. Unless your case is the exception or wisely handled you will see how quickly she makes excuses that she has things she has to do at home.

## A TALEBEARER AND SLANDERER

Fire and lightning are representative of power throughout the scriptures. Fire out of control consumes great forests. Lightning, when it makes contact, can kill a person, set a house on fire, or ignite a forest fire—*even so is strife!* The talebearing woman is she who tosses a dry branch on a hot bed of coals. The fire that had burned itself down will once again rage.

Often this kind of person does not care who is hurt by her words. Or perhaps she deceives herself into believing she is justified in sharing secrets about anyone or everyone. The fact that she is frustrated,

17

selfish, immature, envious, or full of false pride is what she has not faced up to.

We have all heard a person preface her remarks of tattling or slander with, "Have you heard?" "Would you believe?" "Keep this to yourself, but..." Such remarks are designed to fortify the teller in case she is put on the carpet later, but more likely is used as a warning to the hearer to not repeat the gossip. How about the person who assured you that you were the only one she was telling, then in no time at all it began to come to you through other people?

We all need a friend or two to whom we can confide our deep heartaches and concerns. At the same time, we need to know they will keep our concerns confidential as long as we ask so as to not add to our problems. How many of us have a truly trustworthy friend other than our mother or daughter? We should be able to bear one another's burdens (Galatians 6:2).

A talebearer does not always want to hurt another person, but often does it through thoughtlessness or weakness. On the other hand, slander is libel. A slanderer defames or maligns another. All of his utterances are false or are misrepresentations. They are intended to be a stumbling block and offensive. So, even though talebearing may not be intentionally slanderous, it will no doubt have the same effects as slander after being repeated through several individuals.

Listening to gossip and slander and passing it on is a big aid to the devil's destructive work. God has given warning that we cannot bless God and curse man for "out of the abundance of the heart the mouth speaketh." "Speak evil of no man" (Matthew 12:34b; Titus 3:2).

A FALSE WITNESS AND A LIAR

In a few short seconds a malicious lie can throw a dark shadow across the pathway of a completely innocent person which could plague her the rest of her life. Time and ten thousand words of explanation can never completely undo the harm done and the fact that the lie was told.

Jesus, being an Israelite, strictly kept the Old Testament law to perfection. One of those laws was "Thou shalt not bear false witness against thy neighbor" (Exodus 20:15). Yet, Jesus was sentenced to death on the testimony of false witnesses and liars. "Now the chief priests and elders, and all the council, sought false witness against Jesus to put him to death, but found none: Yea, though many false witnesses came, yet found they none. At the last came two false witnesses" (Matthew 26:59,60).

Stephen was stoned to death, the innocent victim of false witnesses.

"And they set up false witnesses which said, This man ceaseth not to speak blasphemous words against this holy place and the law" (Acts 6:13).

There are no "little white lies and big black lies." One is a lie as much as the other. We cannot retell a lie if we refuse to hear it in the first place. Also, how can we know if we are being whispered a lie or the truth? Why do we pass on tales we do not know to be true and most likely do not ourselves believe? If we are listening to every tale and eager to participate in mischief there is little doubt that we will even attempt to keep it quiet.

Paul was the victim of those very people who should have been his most faithful supporters in spreading the gospel. Is this not sometimes true today? "And when he was come, the Jews which came down from Jerusalem stood around about, and laid many and grievous complaints against Paul, which they could not prove" (Acts 25:7). These accusers had sought Paul before, hoping for a chance to kill him on his way to Jerusalem. Insted, he was held at Caesarea and they came down from Jerusalem hoping for an opportunity to destory him. These complaints eventually led to his death in Rome, for he asked to be judged in Rome by Caesar.

The apostle John said of a liar, "The truth is not in him. If we say we have no sin, we deceive ourselves and the truth is not in us" (1 John 2:4; 1:8).

A liar and false witness must be about gathering wood to keep the fire burning. She fuels the fire with tales and lies she has heard and spread then flames leap and get out of control. Just so is the confusion and strife caused by false witnesses and liars.

## A BOASTER

How badly we all need praise and encouragement! It bolsters our confidence and renews our enthusiasm. It helps us tremendously to continue in patience, love and our search for righteousness. How disheartened we would become if we never received commendation and praise. However, most of us want more praise than is good for us, which adds to our vanity, of which we already have too much. So, many times, we throw out our own little boasts and brags, which would be better left unsaid.

A boaster is a selfish, self-centered person and desires always to focus more attention upon himself. How wonderful it would be if we would always stop and think before boasting about ourselves and turn the remark to praise of another's good qualities or works.

# A FLATTERER WITH A FALSE SHOW OF AFFECTION

"Faithful are the wounds of a friend, but the kisses of an enemy are deceitful" (Proverbs 27:6). Undoubtedly, Peter thought he had to withdraw from dining with the Gentiles to keep in good standing with those Jewish Christians who came with Paul. There is no doubt that Paul wounded Peter's pride when he withstood him to the face in the presence of these Jewish Christians. In spite of the fact that Paul did not enhance Peter's self-image but rather told him he was wrong, they remained close friends (Galatians 2:11-14).

"He that blesseth his friend with a loud voice rising early in the morning, it shall be counted a curse to him" (Proverbs 27:14). We have all enjoyed the friendly gatherings after dismissal of our worship services. We have all received a "holy kiss" from someone who was passing them out freely. Not that there is anything wrong with this if the motive is from love and purity. But watch out for the person who is passing out loud compliments at the same time. It does not make any difference what the compliment—if it is loud enough for many to hear, it has achieved its intended purpose.

Sometimes this type of person is entirely different when alone with the person she compliments so loudly. Her need is not always to impress the individual but the majority. The deceitful Judas kiss! The loud compliment! What detestable false shows of affection.

"Rising early in the morning blessing his neighbor with a loud voice" (Proverbs 27:14) reminds us of the loud-mouthed neighbors who get up early on the rare occasions we get a chance to sleep in. My! How the sweet words of nothings pass from yard to yard. The sweetness is piercing and not welcome at this time of day. Likewise, the false flatterer should not be enjoyed.

20

# For Private Meditation
# Or Class Discussion

A CONTENTIOUS PERSON

1. "Only by _____ cometh contention" (Proverbs 13:10a).
2. When contention breaks forth it is as a fire that at first has been gently lit with small kindling; but when larger fuel is added, the flames will begin to leap. "As coals are to _____; and wood to _____; so is a contentious person to _____" (Proverbs 26:21).
3. In what way is a contentious, angry woman like the falling of rain on a very rainy day? _____ (Proverbs 21:19; 27:15).
4. To the Corinthian church Paul wrote, "It has been declared unto me of you...that there are contentions among you." After a discussion of the subject, his summation was, "Ye are yet _____, with _____, _____ and _____" (1 Corinthians 1:11; 3:3).

AN ANGRY AND WRATHFUL PERSON

1. An angry and wrathful person will stir up what? (Proverbs 15:18).
2. To what is this person compared in Proverbs 30:33?
3. How do they stir up anger? (Proverbs 15:1b).
4. How do we know there is a time to get angry?
5. _____ stirreth up strife, and a _____ aboundeth in _____.(Proverbs 29:22).
6. A hot-tempered person rarely thinks before lashing out with foolish, hurtful words or deeds. So, "he that is _____ is of _____: and he that is _____ of spirit _____" (Proverbs 14:29).
7. "See thou a man that is _____? There is more _____ for a fool than for him" (Proverbs 29:20).
8. "He that is soon angry _____" (Proverbs 14:17a).
9. When we are angry, we must guard against what and deal with it how? (Ephesians 4:26).
10. how does a discreet person handle anger?
    a. (Proverbs 19:11).
    b. (Proverbs 16:32).
    c. (Proverbs 15:1).

21

## A BUSY BODY AND A MEDDLER

1. Discuss and apply to today's society Proverbs 25:17 which says, "Withdraw thy foot from thy neighbor's house, lest he be weary of thee and so hate thee." Is this as true today as it was in the days of Solomon?
2. How are we to deal with anyone who wastes our time and meddles in our affairs?
3. Is it possible that we can help the person mentioned in question number two grow up by handling her gently and wisely? In all probability she does not realize the time she is wasting is hers as well as yours. A real friendship could be salvaged and developed into a beautiful relationship. Discuss some ways of dealing with this sort of a neighbor.
4. What is the cure for being idle?
5. What is the cure for being a meddler?
6. What is wrong with being a busybody? What does she do wrong?
7. What are the things busybodies and meddlers speak which they ought not?

## A TALEBEARER AND A SLANDERER

1. How can we avoid the temptation of gossip in the first place?
2. Which is the best, prevention or cure?
3. How much truth should we place on the vast majority of gossip and slanderous reports which we hear?
4. According to James 3:8—"The tongue is a restless evil full of _____."
5. According to James 1:26—"If any man among you seem to be religious and _____, but deceiveth his own heart, this man's religion is _____."
6. "She that goeth about as a talebearer_____" (Proverbs 20:19a).
7. She that repeateth a matter separateth chief friends" (Proverbs 17:9). Could this ever be deliberate?
8. Can listening to the gossip or slander affect my relationship with victim, even if I do not pass it on? How?
9. Did you ever have anyone reveal a secret of yours in jest? If so, how did you feel about it?
10. What is the difference in gossip and slander?
11. Is slander always damaging?
12. What are some excuses a person would use for slandering another? What are the real reasons?
13. After a vision in which he saw the Lord, Isaiah said, "Woe is

22

me! for I am undone: for I am a man of_____, and I live in the midst of people with _____, then the Lord took away his iniquity and purged his sins'' (Isaiah 6:5a).

14. In what way is Isaiah's example one that we should follow in seeking help from our problems with the tongue?

## A FALSE WITNESS AND A LIAR

1. What is a witness? What is a false witness?
2. "A false witness uttereth _____'' (Proverbs 14:5b).
3. "A false witness _____'' (Proverbs 12:17b).
4. How long does it take to tell a lie? (Proverbs 12:19b). A lying tongue _____.''
5. How long does it take to undo the damage caused by a lie?
6. "A liar gives ear to _____'' (Proverbs 17:4).
7. "A false witness _____ and he that speaketh lies _____'' (Proverbs 19:9; Revelation 20:10; 21:8).
8. Paul told Titus "to speak evil of no man" (Titus 3:2). Here are some well-known scriptures that will help us avoid using our tongue in this way:
   a. Philippians 4:8
   b. John 13:34-35
   c. James 4:7

## A BOASTER

1. "Even so the tongue is a _____ and _____ _____'' (James 3:5a).
2. "All the _____''(Psalms 94:4b).
3. Why does one boast according to 2 Timothy 3:2?
4. Do you find it hard to compliment a boaster? Why?
5. Paul foretold Timothy of the perilous times to come in these last days; among those listed with a form of godliness by denying the power of God are boasters. His admonition to us in the last verse is what? (2 Timothy 3:1,2,5).
6. King David asked a question which I have asked myself many times. "Lord, how long shall the wicked triumph?" "how long shall they _____?'' "And all the workers of _____'' (Psalm 94:3,4).
7. "Most men will proclaim every man his _____ but a faithful man who can find? (Proverbs 20:6).
8. Is it not of greater satisfaction in every way when we "Let another man_____, and not_____; a stranger and not

23

_____" (Proverbs 27:2).

9. Some of Jesus' believers failed to confess him because "they loved the praise of _____ more than the praise of God" (John 12:43).

10. Who should we praise first, last and always? "My praise shall be _____ in the great _____" (Psalms 22:25a).

## A FLATTERER WITH A FALSE SHOW OF AFFECTION

1. How can we know if a person's show of affection is false?
2. Did a friend ever wound your feelings? Did it hurt? Did it end your friendship?
3. "Meddle not with him that flattereth with his lips" (Proverbs 20:19b. Why?
4. He that speaketh flattery to his friends, even the eyes of his children shall fail" (Job 17:5). How does this affect the examples we set for our children?

24

Chapter Four
# The Plight of a Person Who Causes Strife

## BECOMES A HYPOCRITE

The person who causes strife can become a hypocrite in all of his ways. The dictionary definition of "hypocrisy" is "a pretense of what one is not." And a hypocrite is "one who puts on a pretense of virtue or qualities he does not have." The original meaning of the word "hypocrite" was "an actor, as on stage playing a role."

There are many biblical instances of hypocrisy:

1. Jacob impersonated Esau when he approached their father Isaac to receive the blessing. When Isaac asked him if he were Esau he answered, "I am" (Genesis 27:24).

2. Jacob's sons took Joseph's coat, dipped it in goat's blood and took it to their father saying, "This we have found; know now whether it is thy son's coat or no. And Jacob knew it was his son's. And he mourned for him many days" (Genesis 37:31-34).

3. Job had much to say about hypocrites. The three friends who came to comfort him in his sufferings of pain and sorrow contended that his suffering was because of a gross sin he had committed. They urged him to confess this great sin and repent. But this was not the case with righteous Job. The three would-be comforters assumed that they appeared to be virtuous and righteous, but they were hypocrites.

4. Isaiah spoke for God regarding the chosen people of his time and those to follow when he prophesied, "They draw near me with their mouth, and with their lips do honor me, but have removed their hearts far from me" (Isaiah 29:13).

5. Jesus quoted Isaiah's prophesy to the offspring of those same people, the Israelites, saying, "Ye HYPOCRITES, well did Isaiah prophesy of you, saying, this people draweth nigh unto me with their

25

mouth, and honoreth me with their lips; but their heart is far from me'' (Matthew 15:7,8).

6. King Herod revealed his hypocrisy to the wise men when he sent them to search for baby Jesus, saying, ''When you find him bring me word that I may come and worship him also.'' In reality King Herod wanted him found that he could have him killed (Matthew 2:8,16).

## BECOMES A SCORNER

A scorner is a person full of hate; one who rejects God and his children with vigorous anger and contempt. A scorner holds all who are just and holy in contempt. He mocks their judgment and God's threatenings and judgments against sinners. He is scornful of wholesome reproofs and counsels.

A scorner is selfish and loves himself above all other persons and things. He thinks himself to be kept above the other person by whatever means of scorn he can employ. It may be by a vague, belittling remark or by strong, snarling pronouncements or by a quiet, sullen, hateful type of treachery. Whatever the means, he is led to proud wrath (Proverbs 21:24).

A scorner has no understanding of things holy nor of the righteousness of God's people. He will scoff at or make mock of sin (in particular those sins of which he is the most guilty).

Job had friends of this caliber. He recognized their sins of attitude and word. He asked God, ''Are there not mockers with me? For thou hast hid their hearts from understanding; therefore shalt thou not exalt them'' (Job 17:2,4). These friends of suffering Job were not wise, and so were not aware of what they were doing to him. They did not know that they were criticizing him with scorn and foolishness. ''Scornful men bring a city into a snare (set a city aflame): but wise men turn away wrath'' (Proverbs 29:8). It begins with just a tiny spark and the majestic trees of a great forest are destroyed. In just such a way is a person disfigured and scarred and perhaps forever lost by the damage done by scorners. This is especially true of youth.

We all know how it hurts to be made fun of, torn apart, mocked and belittled—to become the target of a scorner. The cares of life are heavy enough without any downgrading. David experienced this type of persecution. He had to hide in the mountains and caves to save his life when Saul, in his fits of envy and proud wrath, sought to kill him. David later wrote, ''Our soul is exceedingly filled with the scorning of those that are at ease: and with the contempt of the proud'' (Psalms 123:4).

It is very easy when one is in good health, prospering, and free of

26

worry and anxiety to scoff at those of apparent less good fortune. But, let us reconsider, for everyone has times of sickness, death of a loved one, anxieties of all sorts before this life is ended. Beware, unless the Lord says to us (as he did to those who would not listen and profit by his counsel and reproofs) "When wisdom crieth out in the streets...how long will the scorners delight in their scorning?...I will laugh at your calamity; I will mock when your fear cometh" (Proverbs 1:12). But as in all instances we are free agents to listen to wisdom, to choose the way leading to peace and salvation. Then, as Solomon said in conclusion to these admonitions, "Whosoever hearkeneth unto me shall dwell safely, and shall be quiet from fear of evil" (Proverbs 1:20-33).

Jude wrote of the words of the apostles of the Lord, saying, "How that they told you there should be mockers in the last time, who would walk after their own ungodly lusts. These are they who separate themselves, sensual, having not the Spirit" (Jude 17-19).

## BECOMES AN UNJUST VENGEFUL PERSON

The Old Law, which we think of as "an eye for an eye and a tooth for a tooth," was given before mankind was prepared to walk by faith. It was a physical law where they had to see the results to learn the lesson intended (Exodus 21:24,25; Leviticus 24:17-21; Deuteronomy 19:16-21). The idea was to do to the offender what the offender did to another. This is stated in the law: "A life for a life, an eye for an eye, a tooth for a tooth, a hand for a hand, a foot for a foot, AND THOSE WHICH REMAIN SHALL HEAR AND FEAR, AND SHALL HENCEFORTH COMMIT NO MORE ANY SUCH EVIL AMONG YOU." (Deuteronomy 19:20).

Paul said of Sodom and Gomorrah, "They are set for an example, suffering the vengeance of eternal fire" (Jude 7).

Some people of our day contend that the death sentence is a deterrent to crime. Did knowing that the law said, "A life for a life" act as a deterrent to Judas when he betrayed Christ?

Since the advent of the Christian Age it is said, "To repay evil with evil is of the devil; to repay good for good is human, but to repay evil with good is of God."

To "get even" with another person for the evil he has done you comes from hate, bitterness, resentment and a lack of forgiveness. God does not tolerate those qualities in his people. Also, if we find ourselves a target for this kind of a person, we must "say not thou, I will recompense evil for evil, but wait on the Lord and he shall save thee" (Proverbs 20:22).

27

Jesus said in his great teachings in the beginning of his ministry, "Ye have heard that it hath been said, 'An eye for an eye, and a tooth for a tooth;' but I say unto you, That ye resist not him that is evil: but whosoever shall smite thee on the right cheek, turn to him the other also" (Matthew 5:38-42). "Do good to them that hate you, pray for them which despitefully use you; to him that smite thee on one cheek offer also the other" (Luke 6:27).

These words Jesus spoke are a vital part of the Christian life. He said, "As ye would that men should do to you, do ye also to them likewise" (Luke 6:31). Then He stated the reason for his teaching when he said, "The sinners love those that love them, and sinners do good to them which do good to them; sinners lend to sinners to receive as much again" (Luke 6:32-34). Christ suffered wrong, for us. He is our example. He did not revile nor threaten when he was reviled and suffering.

Two people with opposite moral and spiritual values cannot sufficiently understand each other to be always fair and just in their dealings with each other. Their very differences will cause emotional upheavals. This makes a calm, peaceful and close friendship almost impossible. For, some time in some way, wrath will give way to vengeance. With emotions under pressure, the volcano will erupt. We should avoid these pressures as much as possible.

Many times the underlying cause of vengeance is jealousy. Anyone who deliberately provokes the jealousy of another person is asking for trouble. But an unjust person will be jealous of everyone that has more or does more than they, so if we are wise we will avoid keeping constant company with this type of a person. We will know if a person does not treat us right and we will not be comfortable in the situation. This does not give us the right to "get even" by mistreating them. These facts are taught in the following Proverbs:

"An unjust person is abomination to the just" (29:27a).

"For jealousy is the rage of a man; therefore he will not spare in the day of vengeance. He will not regard any ransom; neither will he rest content though thou givest many gifts" (6:34,35).

However, with the Lord's help we will be able to accept and tolerate this kind of a person. We will always be able to do to them as we would have them do to us (with God's assistance).

By way of summary, let us conclude that we need have no fear of being guilty of rendering vengeance to anyone if we always practice the Golden Rule. "For all the law is fulfilled in one word, even in this, Thou shalt love thy neighbor as thyself" (Galatians 5:14). So, by loving all persons and treating them kindly and patiently, praying, and rendering good for evil we know we are pleasing to the Lord. Knowing this, we are confident we shall receive the blessings he has promised; not only peace of mind in this life but an eternity of peace and joy with our Father in heaven.

# For Private Meditation
# Or Class Discussion

BECOMES A HYPOCRITE

1. Jesus said, "Woe unto you, scribes and Pharisees, _____, for ye pay tithes of mint, anise and cumin, and have omitted the weightier matters of the law, _____, _____ and _____; these ought ye to have done, and not to leave the other undone" (Matthew 23:23).
   a. Jesus again calls them "hypocrites" and compares them to _____, which indeed appear beautiful outward, but are within full of _____ and of all _____ (Verse 27).
   b. A hypocrite outwardly appears to be righteous, but Jesus said, "Within ye are_____" (Verse 28).
   c. Jesus also called them what kind of Pharisees? (Verse 26).
2. Does a hypocrite know he is a hypocrite?
3. Do we spot hypocrites readily? How can we know one?
4. Are there hypocrites in your congregation?
5. Do we stay away from services to avoid being with hypocrites?
6. Do we stay away from family or community affairs to avoid being with hypocrites?
7. Solomon said, "Burning lips and a wicked heart are like an earthen vessel _____" (Proverbs 26:23).
8. "But the hypocrites in heart_____" (Job 36:13a).
9. "A hypocrite with his mouth_____" (Proverbs 11:9a).
10. "Their tongue is as an _____, it speaketh _____; one speaketh peaceably to his neighbor with his mouth, but in his heart _____" (Jeremiah 9:8).
11. Jesus said, "The hypocrites love to pray _____, and in the _____ that they may be _____" (Matthew 6:5). Jesus warned that we be not like them!
12. "The triumphing of the wicked is _____, and the joy of the hypocrite is _____" (Job 20:5).
13. What did Jesus tell the hypocrites to do to remedy their blindness? (Matthew 7:5).

BECOMES A SCORNER

1. What kind of persons make a mock of sin? (Proverbs 14:9).

2. Peter said scoffers walk after what? (2 Peter 3:3).
3. How does a scorner feel about his scorning? "The scorner ____"
   (Proverbs 1:22b).
4. When Job was suffering, his friends mocked him. What was
   his reaction? "My friends scorn me, but _____"
   (Job 16:20).
5. Can a scorner find wisdom? If not, why not? "A scorner seeketh
   wisdom, but_____:
   but _____" (Proverbs 14:6).
6. Why do we allow scorners to continue hurting others? Could it
   be because we fear their animosity? The Proverbs say:
   a. "Reprove not a scorner _____" (9:8a; 15:12).
   b. "He that reproveth a scorner_____" (9:7a).
7. Does it do any good to reprove a scorner? "A scorner
   _____" (Proverbs 13:1b).
8. Does anyone take sides with a scorner? "If thou scornest ____"
   (Proverbs 9:12b).
9. Should scorners be punished? If so, how? and what good will it
   do? "Smite a scorner and_____"
   (Proverbs 19:25). "When the scorner is punished, the _____"
   (Proverbs 21:11).
10. When a scorner is cast out, what are the results?
    (Proverbs 22:10):
    a. "Cast out the scorner and _____."
    b. "Yea _____."
11. What is the destiny of a scorner? (Proverbs 19:29). Does this
    mean we are to judge whether the individual is lost or saved?
    "For the terrible one is brought to naught and the scorner is
    _____" (Isaiah 29:20).

BECOMES AN UNJUST, VENGEFUL PERSON

1. Who will render vengeance?
   a. "Recompense to no man _____" (Romans 12:17a).
   b. "Dearly beloved, avenge not yourselves, but give place unto
      wrath; for it is written _____,
      saith the Lord" (Romans 12:19).
2. According to what will the Lord judge? (1 Peter 1:17; Revelation
   20:12b; 22:12).
3. How and when will the unjust be punished? "The Lord knoweth
   how to deliver the godly out of temptations, and to _____"
   (2 Peter 2:9). "When the Lord Jesus shall be revealed from
   heaven with his mighty angels, in flaming fire,_____

31

and that '' (2 Thessalonians 1:7,8). "But the _____ and the _____ and the _____, and _____, and _____ and _____, and _____ and _____, shall have their part in _____ and _____: which is the _____'' (Revelation 21:8).
4. How are we to react when we are mistreated, and what will be our reward? "Finally, be ye all of one mind, having compassion one for another, love as brethren, be pitiful, be courteous: _____, or _____ (scorn); but CONTRARIWISE _____, knowing that _____, that ye should _____'' (1 Peter 3:8,9).

Chapter Five
# The Plight of a Person
# Who Causes Strife, Continued

The first record of human sin shows that sin was caused by a deceiver in the beginning. Satan deceived Eve in the garden of Eden by lying to her. She was deceived because she believed his lies and acted on them (Genesis 3:1-6).

David said of the ones who sought to destroy him by deceit and treachery, "Thou givest thy mouth to evil, and thy tongue frameth deceit. Thou lovest all devouring words, O thou deceitful tongue. They that speak my hurt speak mischievous things, and imagine deceits all the day long" (Psalms 50:19; 52:4; 38:12b).

A deceitful person is one who leads himself or another person to believe something that is false. This seduction is accomplished in several different ways: by lying, cheating, or beguiling by misleading representations. Such a person has the habit of trying to cover up truth or to twist it, or to give the wrong impression by any devious means. A deceiver is, as Satan, subtle, crafty, cunning, sly or tricky.

Deceivers were not reserved for the first age of mankind. For Paul wrote Timothy that "evil men and seducers shall wax worse and worse, deceiving, and being deceived" (2 Timothy 3:13). When we deceive another person we deceive ourselves also. For a deceiver thinks he has out smarted another. This is true whether or not he realizes what he is doing. This is also true of groups of people and even of nations.

It seems to be a fact of life that people with too much self-esteem get their feelings hurt sooner or later by some obstacle in their pathway. These obstacles prove whether or not one's faith is strong enough to continue in her commitments. The Jews, blinded by their great pride, deceived themselves by rejecting Christ. To them he was the stumbling block to their salvation. Our faith is proved continually by the obstacles we overcome which we do not allow to deceive us or become a stumbling block.

Peter truly believed he would never deny knowing Jesus, for he said, "Though I should die with thee yet I will not deny thee." Yet he was deceiving himself—for when he was put to the test he fell short (Matthew 26:33,34).

Although Peter became strong and learned to guard his tongue against deceit and to overcome evil with good, he had to suffer for his deceit. We will suffer in this life from our deceitful ways just as Peter did. We may fool ourselves but we never fool God. Solomon, in his wisdom, saw repayment in suffering for one's own deceit. He said, "Bread of deceit is sweet to a man; but afterwards his mouth shall be filled with gravel" (Proverbs 20:17).

## BECOMES A SOWER OF DISCORD

One who sows discord among the brethren is one who causes strife, and strife causes division. None of us admire nor want to be this kind of person. Yet, when one becomes a hypocrite, a scorner, a deceiver, a meddler, a talebearer, a slanderer, a false witness or a liar and will not accept instruction and correction, that person will by these very means be a sower of discord among his Christian brethren. A person whose heart is rebellious and seeks mischief, continually sowing discord, has blinded his heart to the fact that he is destructive. Such a one includes himself in his own path of destruction.

"The start of dissention is like the first break in a dam: stop it before it goes any further" (Proverbs 17:14—paraphrased). Just because something is the truth does not automatically give us the right to publish it. If we take even a moment to think of the end results of careless words and the possible position into which we put ourselves, we would be much less apt to reveal secrets.

When we learn to exercise self-control in the use of the words which we speak, we will have learned to avoid continual turmoil in our own life as well as in the lives of others. James said, "Behold, how much wood a little fire kindleth. And the tongue is a fire, a world of iniquity: so is the tongue among our members that it defiles the whole body, and sets on fire the course of nature, and it is set on fire of hell" (James 3:5b, 6).

A rapid, honest self-examination before we speak reveals to us the intent of our heart—whether it intends good or evil. Too, if we delay speaking long enough, we may realize the possible end results. Knowing we could be put on the witness stand to affirm every word we have spoken we would have less trouble in curbing our words.

34

## THE SEEDS OF DISCORD

The Kind of Person that Sows Them:

These six things doth the Lord hate: Yea, seven are an abomination unto Him: A proud look, a lying tongue, and hands that shed innocent blood, an heart that deviseth wicked imaginations, feet that be swift in running to mischief, a false witness that speaketh lies, and he that soweth discord among the brethren" (Proverbs 6:16-19).

Since the Lord hates six things, but seven are an abomination unto him, do you think the Lord does not hate one of the abominations? Of course you do not think that! Could it be that the seventh abomination is the end result of each of the others?

## WHAT IS TO BE DONE WITH SOWERS OF DISCORD?

Of those who taught false doctrine, thus causing discord, Paul wrote to the church at Rome, "Now I beseech you brethren, mark them which cause divisions and offences contrary to the doctrine which ye heard (learned), and avoid them" (Romans 16:17).

Concerning those guilty of any of the seven abominations named in Proverbs 6, Paul wrote to Titus saying, "A man that is a factious man after the first and second admonition reject, knowing that he that is such is subverted and sinneth, being condemned of himself" (Titus 3:10,11).

Jesus taught his disciples how to deal with each other in cases of offense or sin against each other. Let us discuss the steps to be taken in order to avoid disturbing the peace of mind we all desire to maintain throughout our lives. Insofar as is possible, prevent strife and division from occurring. This could most often be achieved if we would but follow the steps Jesus commanded his disciples to follow (Matthew 18:15-17).

## OVERCOMING STRIFE, DISCORD AND DIVISION

Paul wrote to the church at Corinth saying, "It has been declared unto me that there are contentions among you..." Then he asked the all-important question "is Christ divided?" Then he beseeched them in the name of the Lord Jesus Christ,"That ye speak the same things, and that there be no divisions among you: but that ye be perfectly joined together in the same mind and in the same judgment (1 Corinthians 1:11, 13; 1:10; cf. Mark 9:50; Hebrews 12:14; Romans 12:19-21; Titus 3:8).

35

# For Private Meditation
# Or Class Discussion

BECOMES A DECEIVER

1. Satan, the Great Deceiver:
   a. In the Garden of Eden, was Adam deceived by Satan? (1 Timothy 2:14,15).
   b. If Adam was not deceived, did he sin? If so, in what way?
   c. How successful has Satan been in continuing to deceive people? (Revelation 12:9; 13:14, 18:23).
2. Ways in which we deceive ourselves:
   a. "If a man _____ when he is _____, he deceiveth himself" (Galatians 6:3).
   b. "If any man among you seem to be religious and _____, but deceiveth his own heart, this man's religion is _____" (James 1:26).
   c. "He that passeth by, and meddleth with strife belonging not to him, is like one that _____. As a ____ so is the man that deceiveth his neighbor, and saith, '_____?' " (Proverbs 26:17-19).
   d. "Be ye _____, and _____, deceiving your own selves" (James 1:22).
3. The results of deception:
   a. "Bread of deceit is _____, but afterwards _____" (Proverbs 20:17).
   b. "Be not deceived; _____: For whatsoever a man _____, that shall he also _____" (Galatians 6:7).
   c. "Know ye not that the unrighteous_____? Be not deceived..." (1 Corinthians 6:9a).
4. Overcoming deception:
   a. Jesus warned his followers, " _____ that ye be not deceived..." (Luke 21:8a).
   b. "With Him is strength and wisdom. The deceived and the deceiver_____" (Job 12:16). "O that ye would altogether _____! And it should be _____" (Job 13:5).
   c. "In your patience ye shall _____" (Luke 21:19).

36

## SIX THINGS THE LORD HATES

1. A proud look
   "The wicked _____ will not
   seek after God: God is not in all his thoughts" (Psalms 10:4).
2. A lying tongue
   a. "Ye shall not steal, neither deal falsely, neither _____
      (Leviticus 19:11).
   b. David prayed, "Deliver my soul, O Lord, _____
      My soul hath long dwelt with him that hateth peace. I am for
      peace; but when I speak they are for war" (Psalms
      120:2, 6, 7).
3. Hands that shed innocent blood
   a. "Manasseh shed innocent blood very much, _____"
      (2 Kings 21:16a).
   b. "If ye shed not innocent blood in this place, then will I cause
      you _____" (Jeremiah 7:6,7).
   c. "Egypt shall be a desolation, and Edom shall be a desolate
      wilderness, _____, because
      they have shed innocent blood in their land" (Joel 3:19).
   d. "Thou shalt destroy them that speak lies: _____
      the bloody and deceitful man" (Psalms 5:6).
4. A heart that deviseth wicked imaginations
   a. "Frowardness is in his heart, _____;
      he soweth discord" (Proverbs 6:14).
   b. "He that is_____ stirreth up strife;
      but he that putteth his trust in the Lord shall be made fat"
      (Proverbs 28:25).
   c. "He is proud, knowing nothing, but _____,
      whereof cometh envy, strife, railings, evil surmisings"
      (1 Timothy 6:4).
   d. "But_____ knowing
      that they do gender strife" (2 Timothy 2:23).
5. Feet that run to mischief
   a. The Lord spoke unto Moses, "Thou shalt not go up and
      down as_____" (Leviticus 19:16a).
   b. "The Lord _____ feet that be swift to running to
      mischief" (Proverbs 6:18b).
   c. "Their feet are swift to shed blood: and the _____
      have they not known" (Romans 3:15,17).
6. False witnesses that speak lies
   a. "Thou shalt not _____" (Exodus 20:16).

b. "A false witness will _____; a deceitful witness _____" (Proverbs 14:5b; :25b).
c. "Be thou not a witness against thy neighbor _____, and deceive not _____" (Proverbs 24:28).
d. "A false witness _____, and he that speaketh lies _____" (Proverbs 19:9).
e. "Deliver me not over to _____; for false witnesses are risen up against me, and such as _____" (Psalms 27:12; Read verses 11 and 14 for encouragement).
7. God hates him that "_____" (Proverbs 6:19b).

## WHAT IS TO BE DONE WITH SOWERS OF DISCORD?

1. What are the 3 steps to be taken? If he shall hear you, what have you gained?
2. If he shall not hear you, what is the next thing to do?
3. If he will not hear the witnesses, what is to be done then? If he refuses to heed any of the three steps taken, what is the relationship between the two of you to be? Do you then treat him as an enemy or a stranger?

Chapter Six
# What Injury is Done
# The Victim of Strife?

## CAUSES OF INJURY

Everything which causes strife is injurious to the individual thus to groups of individuals. We have studied some of the causes of strife, those being: the stresses of everyday living, fears and worries, self-pity, foolishness, pride and envy. The end results of careless words and/or actions are the injuries which have been inflicted. Since strife is a work of the flesh and not a fruit of the spirit, all means of inflicting injury, ruin, even death, are used by the destroyer. These are plainly and simply the tools of the devil; specifically accomplished by the use of the tongue and by actions.

James likens the tongue to a fire. Thus, a tiny spark, fanned by gossip, is a widespread, sweeping power of evil. How sickening is the sight of fire-blackened hills and grotesquely jutting stubs of burned trees where rolling green hills and a pine forest once stood. A city ravaged by fire which leaves countless homes destroyed in its path is terrible. The carelessness of tossing one lighted match or cigarette, or leaving an unsnuffed campfire, may start a raging inferno. But there is a destructive power even greater than these—that of the unguarded tongue.

There are actions which can hurt as severely as words. It is easier to combat physical attack than silent disdain—for what tactics does one use against silence? A person treated in this manner is affected deeply by being ignored or snubbed, or by any other means shown a lack of due respect, concern and love.

## INJURY TO THE VICTIM

Any injury results in hurt feelings—this affects one's own self-esteem. One's reputation may be damaged or ruined, which greatly curtails his ability to be useful.

If we even listen to gossip it has a detrimental effect on us. There is always a shadow of doubt cast as to the amount of truth in gossip. So, without realizing it, we think a little less of the victim of gossip than we had before. This is a particular hardship to leaders. Sometimes the damage done is unsurmountable, hampering, or it may even end an effective work and influence. The results may be a soul charred for eternity.

A VICTIM OF ENVY

Jesus was the world's most innocent and upright victim of envy. He stood before the governor on trial for his life. Pilate knew that for envy the people had delivered Jesus to be crucified rather than the prisoner Barabbas. (Matthew 27:15-26). The true nature of envy can be seen in these two passages: "He that is upright in the way is an abomination to the wicked" (Proverbs 29:27b) and "Wrath is cruel and anger is outrageous; but who is able to stand before envy?" (Proverbs 27:4).

When Joseph's brothers saw that their father had more love for Joseph than for them they hated their brother. The hatred grew more intense due to Joseph's two dreams in which the brothers bowed down to him as to one who ruled over them. His brothers envied him. They cast him into a pit; then sold him to Ishmaelites traveling to Egypt. In Egypt he was sold to the captain of the guard of Pharaoh. (Genesis 37:27,28).

A victim of envy can be cruelly wounded, ruined or even put to death. A person's influence can be damaged in several ways. One way is by losing confidence in self and in others, as well as losing respect. A second damage to influence is a loss of reputation to some degree. Third, influence can be damaged by the loss of opportunities that were available before.

Gossip and talebearing are perhaps the greatest weapons of injury used to hurt the victim of envy. They do hurt deeply; any defense against gossip and talebearing cannot erase the damage done whether the tale is true or not. Solomon said, "The words of a talebearer are as wounds, they go down into the innermost parts of the body" (Proverbs 26:22). Hate is the father of lies, so if one tells something that is untrue about another he is setting up a situation that is impossible to deal with. "A lying tongue hateth those that are afflicted by it" (Proverbs 26:28a).

## A VICTIM OF BETRAYAL

Jesus was, is and always will be the world's most innocent victim of betrayal. "Now (Judas) that betrayed him gave this sign saying, 'whomsoever I shall kiss that same is he, hold him fast.' And forthwith he came to Jesus and said, 'Hail, Master,' and kissed him. And Jesus said unto him, 'Friend, wherefore art thou come?' Then came they and laid hands on Jesus and took him." Jesus had previously said to him, "Judas, betrayest thou the Son of man with a kiss?" (Matthew 26:47-50; Mark 14:43-46; Luke 22:47,48; John 18:3,7). "The kisses of an enemy are deceitful" (Proverbs 27:6b).

There are those like Judas who put on a show of love and affection in public with a kiss and flattering words. We have all had this experience whether aware of it or not. Our trust begins to dim at the time we become aware of the fact that we only receive this devoted attention in a crowd. It really hurts to learn that a friend is not what she appears to be on the surface. Yet let us not judge too quickly nor harshly her motive for such tactics. It could be that she has tried to gain our attention and love and other means have failed. If this is the case, we need to make a change in self. A genuine show of affection may be gained by kind attention and encouragement to someone who needs assurance that they are important to you. But, there are those who do flatter for their own selfish advantage. With a show of love, prayer and God's help, we may be able to change a person's insincerity to truth and love.

## SINNER INJURES SELF MORE THAN HIS VICTIM

We shall reap what we have sown (Galatians 6:7).

The Old Testament gives good farming advice: "Thou shalt not sow thy vineyard with divers seeds: lest the fruit of the seed which thou hast sown and the fruit of the vineyard be defiled" (Deuteronomy 22:9a). The prophet Jeremiah said to those same people, "Break up your fallow ground and sow not among thorns" (Jeremiah 4:3b).

The well-known parable of the sower who went forth to sow, spoken by Jesus to the multitude, told only of the sowing of good seed. The ground in which the seed is sown is what makes the difference. Let us compare the sowing of seed with the sowing of the word of God, the spiritual seed. If the seeds of righteousness are sown in good ground they bring forth good fruit. If sown in stony, sunbaked, hard ground, or among thorns, they will not sink deep enough roots to survive or will be choked out by thorns and weeds, bearing bad fruit or no fruit (Matthew 13:3-8).

41

## LIVES WITH A BAD CONSCIENCE AND REMORSE

If we have sown bad seed in ill-prepared ground, we suffer the consequences of living with bad conscience and remorse. David lived with remorse all the days of his life for the terrible things he had done; yet his good heart and continual repentance made him greatly loved by the Lord. He wrote in Psalms 51:3 "For I acknowledge my transgressions; and my sin is ever before me."

After the cock crowed, Peter realized he had denied the Lord three times. He was filled with remorse and went out and wept bitterly (Matthew 26:75).

David and Peter expressed the remorse, sorrow and suffering they brought on themselves. Because of their penitent hearts they carried on to do great and blessed things for the Lord. David said, "They that sow in tears shall reap in joy. He who goes forth and weeps, bearing precious seed, shall doubtless come again with rejoicing, bringing his sheaves with him" (Psalms 126:5,6).

God forbid that we should fail to repent and ask God to forgive our every sin rather than live with an evil conscience, trying to deceive ourselves and others that we have not sinned. This hardness of heart caused Judas to take his own life. Let us not deceive ourselves when living with a bad conscience, for "if our heart condemn us, God is greater than our heart, and knoweth all things" (1 John 3:20).

## HE THAT LIVES BY THE SWORD SHALL DIE BY THE SWORD

After Peter had drawn his sword and cut off the ear of the servant of the high priest, Jesus said, "Put up again thy sword into its place: for all they that take the sword shall perish with the sword" (Matthew 26:52). "He that leadeth into captivity shall go into captivity: He that killeth with the sword must be killed with the sword... (Revelation 13:10).

The same truth was stated by Job in this way, "Even as I have seen, they that plow iniquity, and sow wickedness shall reap the same" (Job 4:8).

If we live violently we will die violently. If the only seed we sow is to fleshly lusts, the fruit we shall bear will be the fruits of fleshly lusts. "The works of the flesh are these: adultery, fornication, uncleanness, lasciviousness, idolatry, witchcraft, hatred, strife, jealousies, wrath, factions, divisions, heresies, envyings, murders, drunkenness, revelings, and such like; of the which I tell you as I have also told you in time past, that they which do such things shall not inherit the kingdom of God" (Galatians 5:19-21). "He that soweth to the flesh shall of the

42

flesh reap corruption" (Galatians 6:8).

It is for certain if we go through life unconcerned about the injury we inflict upon others we shall pay throughout eternity. We must not conform to this world and its ways or we will be spending eternity in a place far worse than this world.

On the day of judgment let us not hear Jesus say, "Depart from me all ye workers of iniquity. There shall be weeping and gnashing of teeth, when ye shall see Abraham, Isaac and Jacob, and all the prophets in the kingdom of God, and you, yourselves thrust out" (Luke 13:27,28).

Job said, "By the blast of God they perish, by the breath of his nostrils they are consumed. They are destroyed from morning to evening: they perish forever without any regarding" (Job 4:9,20).

## WE MUST RULE OUR THOUGHTS, WORDS AND ACTIONS

We must guard our feelings and dealings with others. We must think and do good. "He that soweth to the Spirit shall of the Spirit reap life everlasting" (Galatians 6:8b).

The righteousness of faith, and how to obtain it, is to be found in the *word of faith*. "...the word is nigh, even in thy mouth, and in thy heart; that is, the word of faith, which we preach; That if thou shall confess with thy mouth the Lord Jesus and shall believe in thine heart that God hath raised Him from the dead, thou shalt be saved. For with the heart man believeth unto righteousness, and with the mouth confession is made unto salvation" (Romans 10:8,9). Solomon quoted God saying that if we reject the words of faith..."Ye have set at naught my counsels...they shall not find me..." (Proverbs 25:28).

When we truly realize the destructive power of sin, we will become equipped with a forceful incentive to be truly righteous. Even the wicked can teach us. "When the wicked are multiplied, trangressions increase...the righteous shall see their fall" (Proverbs 29:16). An object lesson learned is a valuable asset.

Paul's advice is, "Let your speech be always with grace, seasoned with salt, that ye may know how to answer every man" (Colossians 4:6). We must try to come to an understanding with those who are giving us problems and not become discouraged. Our prayer, as David's, should be, "Search me, O God, and know my heart: Try me and know my thoughts and see if there be any wicked way in me, and lead me in the way everlasting" (Psalms 139:23, 24).

43

# For Private Meditation
# Or Class Discussion

CAUSES OF INJURY

1. What are the main tools the devil uses to inflict injury on the victim through us?
2. In James 3:6, the tongue is likened to what?
3. A fire can be very comforting to warm by. At what point does it become dangerous?
4. The tongue can also give comfort, but at what point does it inflict injury?
5. Other than physical actions, what kind of actions hurt as badly as words? Is physical attack easier to combat than silent disdain?
6. How should we deal with each other?

INJURY TO THE VICTIM

1. Is it fair to think less of a person because of some gossip we have heard about him? Discuss this situation.
2. Why did the people demand Jesus be crucified? (Matthew 27:18).
3. Envy is harder to deal with than wrath or anger (Proverbs 27:4). Why is this true?
4. What are three losses the victim of envy can suffer?
5. What has hate to do with lying?
6. What is flattery?
7. Whose heart and actions must we always examine first?
8. How can we help someone to change who is not what they appear on the surface to be?

SINNER INJURES SELF MORE THAN HIS VICTIM

1. Sowing bad seed is equivalent to what?
2. What are the fruits of bad seed?
3. What are the fruits of good seed?
4. What made it possible for both David and Peter to continue on and bear precious fruit for the Lord?
5. Can we live with a bad conscience and be pleasing to God? (1 John 3:20-21).
6. Jesus taught, "He that killeth with the sword must be _____" (Revelation 13:10; cf. Matthew 26:52).

44

7. "He that soweth to the flesh shall of the flesh reap _____."
8. If Jesus says "Depart from me," what will be our destiny? (Galatians 5:8).
9. How can we keep our souls from trouble? (Proverbs 21:23).
10. How can we learn from the wicked? (Proverbs 29:16).

Chapter Seven

# Trust in the Lord

Faith is a monumental kind of trust. A trust that does not say, "I'll trust you when you have fulfilled your promise" but says, "The important thing is that the promises can be anticipated, waited for and believed in; although the fulfillment may be in the life to come." That is where we, as children of God, put our trust, knowing that we will be victorious when the works of this life are rewarded.

On this strange journey God has promised us help for all our needs and will deliver us in times of trouble. But we must do our part with full confidence that God will keep his promise. Paul advised, "Above all, taking the shield of faith, wherewith we shall be able to quench all the fiery darts of the wicked one" (Ephesians 6:16).

David trusted God and did not hesitate to call on him rather than man. He prayed, "O God, give us help from trouble: for vain is the help of man. Through God we shall do valiantly; for He it is that shall tread down our enemies" (Psalms 60:11,12).

God is faithful to his obedient children. With his help we will be able to rise above all temptations; to recognize, evaluate and deal with all our problems. Some problems we will solve by abolishing them and others we will overcome by learning to live peacefully with them. We will learn to know the difference in the things we can change and the things we cannot. With each ordeal we will rise a little higher above strife—for God has promised, "There is no temptation given you but such is as common to man: but God is faithful, who will not suffer you to be tempted above that ye are able, but will with the temptation also make a way of escape, that ye may be able to bear it" (1 Corinthians 10:13).

We needed help and we found it in Jesus. We were hungry and our souls were satisfied. "God hath delivered us from the power of darkness and hath translated us into the kingdom of his dear Son" (Colossians 1:13). If we do not know what to do, God expects us to ask him in prayer without doubting that he will show us the way, guiding us in his love and wisdom.

Even in the midst of adversities there are things that are essential and lasting. Those things give our life meaning and importance. Our choice, like Abraham's, is by faith, "for faith gives us the assurance of things hoped for, and the conviction of things not seen" (Hebrews 1:1).

But how do we get faith? It must be learned and believed. "So then, faith cometh by hearing and hearing by the word of God."

## KEEP BUSY IN SERVICE TO GOD

After experiencing everything this life has to offer, Solomon understood that this is a moral world and there is a judgment to be faced. Solomon also realized that there is a never-ending life, that there is a supreme God and we are responsible to Him. His solution to the problem was, "Fear God and keep his commandments; for this is the whole duty of man. For God shall bring every work into judgment, with every secret thing whether it be good or whether it be evil" (Ecclesiastes 12:13, 14). The apostle Paul said, "We are God's workmanship created in Christ Jesus unto good works—we should walk in them" (Ephesians 2:10).

We are free to make a choice of whether to serve God—to do all to his glory—or to indulge in the selfish, sinful pleasures of this life with no hope of a better life to come.

With the love of Jesus enshrined in our heart, its holy influence will be felt by all with whom we come in contact. It will be like a spring of refreshing water in the desert for those who are thirsty. If we are filled with the righteousness of Christ and the joy of his Spirit, we will want to share this blessing with others—and in so doing we will receive blessings upon ourselves. Those who participate in this labor of love are those who grow to maturity in the grace and knowledge of Christ.

Unselfish labor for others gives depth, stability and loveliness to our character and brings peace and happiness as nothing else can. Those who passively accept the blessings of God's grace and do nothing for Christ are like those who eat without working. There are those who fail to exercise their strength and lose the power they already have.

As in every aspect of life, Jesus is our perfect example. Much of his life was spent working in a carpenter's shop in Nazareth. He was as faithfully fulfilling his mission while working at this humble trade as he was when he healed the sick, fed the 5,000, or walked upon the storm-tossed Sea of Galilee. The work which we do to earn the necessities of life, whether lowly hard labor or the most dignified professional positions in our society, must be as a faithful representative of Jesus Christ, revealing the spirit of Christ which is in us. If this spirit is in us it will be manifest in everything we do and will give us satisfaction and fulfillment.

Why are so many of us consumed with the idea that we should serve God in some special capacity? Not all are given the special aptitude for organizing and conducting workshops or seminars, for teaching a class, for writing a book. Why are we such rebels when it comes to being a lowly servant of the Lord, to serving people who are in dire need? Could it be we do not really believe what Jesus said to James and John who had great ambitions to have a prominent position in the Lord's kingdom? "To the apostles, Jesus called them unto him and said, 'Ye know that the princes of the Gentiles exercise dominion over them and they that are great but whosoever will be chief among you, let him be your servant. Even as the Son of man came not to be ministered unto but to minister and to give his life as ransom for many' " (Matthew 20:25-28).

From those who have many talents much is required. Those who have few are required to use the few. If the Lord gave me only one talent, I am required to develop it and put it to good use serving Him. Only by helping supply mankind's needs can I minister for Christ. I cannot feed Christ meat, give Christ drink, nor put clothes on Christ's back. But Jesus said, "I was hungry and ye gave me meat; I was thirsty and ye gave me drink; I was a stranger and ye took me in; naked and ye clothed me. I was sick and ye visited me; I was in prison and ye came unto me. *Inasmuch as ye have done it unto one of the least of these my brethren, ye have done it unto me*" (Matthew 25:35-36).

A widow is "well reported of for good works if she has brought up children, if she has lodged strangers, if she has washed the saints' feet, if she has relieved the afflicted, if she has diligently followed every good work" (1 Timothy 5:10).

The real test of our faith is by our works. Do I say and do not? Or do I do and let my works speak for me? James says it in this way, "If a brother or sister be naked or destitute of daily food and one of you say to them, 'Depart in peace, be ye warmed and filled,' notwithstanding ye give them not those things which are needful to the body; what doth it profit? For as the body without the spirit is dead so faith without works is dead also" (James 2:15-16, 26; cf. 1 Corinthians 15:58 and Galatians 6:9).

"The Son of man shall come in the glory of His Father with his angels; and then he shall reward every man according to his works" (Matthew 16:27, Revelation 22:12).

"Every man shall receive his own reward according to his own labor" (1 Corinthians 3:8).

# For Private Meditation Or Class Discussion

## TRUST IN THE LORD

1. What gave Abraham the courage to leave his home for an unknown destination?
2. What are the conditions in the world today that seem unsolvable?
3. What would solve all the world's problems and make peace?
4. If we put all our trust in the Lord, do we have a place for worry about the outcome of world conditions and our lives?
5. When we have done all we can to make things better, then what should be our stand?
6. What is faith? (Hebrews 1:1).
7. Does it take patience to trust? Why?
8. Our faith believes that who overcomes the world? (1 John 5:4,5).
9. Did David put his trust in man to overthrow his enemies? (Psalms 60:11, 12).
10. Is God directing our President? (Daniel 2:21; 5:21; 4:17; Romans 13:1). How can we help the President?
11. Is it a sin to be tempted? (1 Corinthians 10:13).
12. How do we overcome temptation? (1 Corinthians 10:13).
13. What is our avenue for going to God for help and guidance? (Matthew 6:6).
14. David said he prayed for what in Psalms 122:6?
15. If we ask, without faith, that our prayer be answered, can we expect guidance? (James 1:6,7,8).
16. Is it reasonable to expect an immediate answer?
17. Some scripture references on trust:
    a. "Whoso putteth his trust in the Lord _____" (Proverbs 29:25b).
    b. "Whoso trusteth in the Lord _____" (Proverbs 16:20b).
    c. What is the victory that overcomes the world? (1 John 5:4,5).

## KEEP BUSY IN SERVICE TO GOD

1. What is our attitude and action when our work is for the Lord? "Commit thy works unto the Lord, and_____" (Proverbs 16:3). "Serve the Lord_____: Come before his

51

presence _____" (Psalms 100:2).
2. Our faith is profitable toward salvation only when it is accompanied by what? (1 Corinthians 13:3).
3. What did Jesus say to the two apostles who wanted to be greatest in the Kingdom of Heaven? And to ambitious Pharisees? (Matthew 20:26-28; Luke 11:43; Matthew 23:4-12; Mark 12:38-40).
4. How do we serve the Lord by doing the following works (by helping those in need)?
   a. Feed—Matthew 25:35; James 2:15,16; Luke 3:11
   b. Give drink—Matthew 25:35
   c. Clothes—Matthew 25:36; Luke 3:11; James 2:15, 16; Acts 9:36,39
   d. Lodge strangers—Matthew 25:35; Hebrews 13:2; Job 32:32; 1 Timothy 5:10
   e. Visit
      (1). The sick—Matthew 25:36, 1 Timothy 5:10
      (2). Those in prison—Matthew 25:36
      (3). The widows and orphans—James 1:27
   f. Wash the feet of saints—1 Timothy 5:10
   g. Show hospitality—Luke 10:38-42; 2 Kings 4:8; 1 Peter 4:9; Acts 16:15,40.
   h. Be a keeper at home—Wife: Ephesians 5:31,33; Colossians 3:18; 1 Peter 3:1; Titus 2:5. Mother: 1 Timothy 5:10-14; Isaiah 66:13
   i. Be a teacher of God's word—Acts 8:3-4; Titus 2:3-5, Acts 18:26; 2 Timothy 1:5; 1 Peter 3:15
5. What were Paul's instructions for well-doing in Galatians 6:9-10? In Hebrews 13:16?
6. If we see someone in need and have no compassion, can the love of God dwell in us? (1 John 3:17).
7. What advice did Paul have for the rich? (1 Timothy 6:17-18).
8. "Bear ye one another's burdens" (Galatians 6:2). How can we do this? Here are some ways:
   a. Be longsuffering; support the weak; encourage the fainthearted; warn them that are unruly (1 Thessalonians 5:14).
   b. Exhort (urge to do good deeds) daily (Hebrews 3:12,13).
   c. Comfort those who are in trouble (2 Corinthians 1:4).
   d. Restore one taken in a fault (Galatians 6:1).
9. What are some of the programs of the church which meet the previously mentioned needs of others?

10. Read Paul's prayer at the close of his letter to the Hebrews. "The peace of God make you perfect in every good work to do his will" (Hebrews 13:20,21).

## Chapter Eight
# Love God, Self, and One Another

"God is love, and he that dwelleth in love dwelleth in God, and God in him" (1 John 4:8,16).

How do we know that God loved us? Because we believe his word and it reveals this truth. "For God so loved the world, that he gave his only begotten son, that whosoever believeth in him should not perish but have everlasting life." Also, "We love God because he first loved us" (John 3:16 and 1 John 4:9, 5:11,12,19,20).

How do we know if we love God? One of Jesus' disciples asked him, "Lord how is it that thou wilt manifest thyself unto us, and not unto the world?" Jesus answered, "If a man love me he will keep my words: and my Father will love him, and we will come unto him, and make our abode with him" (John 14:22,23).

A true love and respect of one's self is essential before we can love anyone else or Jesus would not have answered the rich young ruler as he did. This young man inquired of Jesus what good thing he could do to inherit eternal life. Jesus summed up the laws of the ten commandments, then added, "Thou shalt love thy neighbor as thyself" (Matthew 19:9b). So, if the man did not love and respect himself how could he love his neighbor? If a man does not love and respect himself, how is it possible to love his wife as the scripture teaches he should? (Ephesians 5:28).

If we love God, we also love one another. The apostle John explains it in a logical way: "...he that loveth not his brother whom he hath seen, how can he love God whom he hath not seen?" (1 John 4:20).

Along with the commandment to love God was the new law Jesus revealed to his followers, saying, "This is my commandment, that ye love one another as I have loved you" (John 13:34; 15:12). This principle was the heart of the new law in Christ Jesus. Every principle of

55

Christianity and righteous living is based on love. Our love for each other shows the whole world that we are truly God's children—for Jesus said, "By this shall all men know that ye are my disciples, if ye have love one to another" (John 13:35).

The greatest love we can have is sacrificial. "Greater love hath no man than this, that a man lay down his life for his friends" (John 15:13). Jesus manifested an even greater love when he willingly gave his life for us. Not only for those who loved and followed him, "But God commended his love toward us, in that, while we were yet sinners, Christ died for us . . . when we were enemies we were reconciled to God by the death of his son . . . " (Romans 5:8,10a).

Because of God's love for us while we were yet sinners, Jesus set the example we are to follow. He expects his children to have greater love than the heathen. Jesus taught his disciples to love their enemies, to "bless them that curse you, to pray for them that despitefully use you; for if you love them which love you only, what reward have you? Do not even the publicans the same?" (Matthew 5:44).

WHAT IS LOVE?

Love is the greatest thing in the world: the greatest moving factor. It never fails and lasts throughout eternity; for it is from God (1 Corinthians 13:8,13). Love assures and ensures us that "all things work together for good to them that love God" (Romans 8:28).

All is pretense and vain in religion where there is no love. Carnal love is based on satisfaction of physical desires and does not fill any deep spiritual need. Love is the only thing that binds people together perfectly. For perfection is doing the will of God with love. Paul wrote to the Colossian church, "Above all things, put on love which is the bond of perfection" (Colossians 3:14).

WHAT LOVE IS NOT

One of man's greatest failings is his strivings to do things which he thinks appear great and good in the eyes of others. But those things are profitless and vain unless the heart is full of love and the motive unselfish.

Paul told the Christians of the first century that without love the spiritual gifts would profit them nothing. Also, that giving all they had to feed the poor or going as far as to give their bodies to be burned—as some religious pagan people did as sacrifices in those days—would profit them nothing without love (1 Corinthians 13:1-3).

## CHARACTERISTICS OF LOVE

Love is the cement that holds all life's human relationships together securely. The family, the government, and the church would never be torn asunder if the ingredients outlined in 1 Corinthians 13:4-8 were faithfully adhered to. It can be compared to the ingredients in a cake. When a woman carefully chooses and expertly blends the ingredients in her favorite recipe, the end product will never fail. Likewise, love.

Here is Paul's recipe for love: (1 Corinthians 13:4-8)

"Love suffereth long" (13:4)

a. God is longsuffering. Read Exodus 34:6; Psalms 86:15; Nehemiah 9:6-33; and 2 Peter 3:9. Why is God longsuffering?

b. Jesus was longsuffering. In spite of the hardships and indignities Jesus suffered on this earth, he never gave up fulfilling his mission (Hebrews 2:12). "And the Lord direct your hearts into the love of God, and into the patience of Christ" (2 Thessalonians 3:5).

c. The prophets and apostles learned to be longsuffering. David was trained to deal with the problems, duties and demands of his coming kingship when he patiently and spiritually handled the persecutions dealt him by Saul. He was not a man to ever give up trying to please God. Read James 5:10,11.

d. We must learn to be longsuffering. In the face of disappointments, discouragements, injuries and injustices, we are commanded to endure, to persevere, to be steadfast, slow to anger and slow to avenge ourselves. We must learn that nothing worthwhile was accomplished quickly; that it takes time, effort and steadfastness if we are to succeed (Hebrews 3:6,14). Babies are impatient; they do not want to wait for anything. But they grow rapidly, learn quickly, and do not give up easily. They learn patience and how to wait for what they want.

## LOVE SEEKS NOT HER OWN

It might be helpful to point out the difference in "needs" and "desires." We are prone to want many things, both material and otherwise, that we do not need, and some that are not good for us. We need food, clothing and shelter for bare existence but we are blessed with far more than that. Some of us have far more than is good for us, spiritually speaking.

One of our greatest failings is to want more than we need, and to want it "right now." Lack of patience and the failure to give ourselves time to think and evaluate is the beginning of many marriage problems of our time. The added pressure of society to possess quickly more of this world's goods than we need or can afford adds burdens and stains to other problems and the marriage vows are abandoned. Paul gave wise advice when he said, "Let us lay aside every weight which does so easily beset us, and let us run with patience the race that is set before us" (Hebrews 12:1). One of our greatest blessings is the ability to be content with what we have and to be thankful.

## LOVE IS KIND

There is no characteristic more appreciated than kindness. It has been said that "kindness is a language which the deaf can hear and the blind can see."

At all times, Jesus demonstrated compassion to those who were weak, poor, ignorant. He had the empathy to project himself into their set of circumstances and to feel deeply their condition. Even to his enemies he demonstrated kindness by telling them the truth. The fact that they closed their minds and rejected his words of wisdom does not erase the fact he cared for them. His courage to tell them the truth was in itself an act of kindness.

David knew God would deal kindly with him even in the midst of enemies who sought to take his life. He expressed his faith and thankfulness in Psalms 42:8, "Yet the Lord will command his loving kindness in the daytime, and in the night his song shall be with me, and my prayer unto the God of my life."

It is not difficult for those who are genuinely considerate of others to be kind to everyone, in every circumstance. One who has both sympathy and empathy can never be cruel nor unkind.

Most of us have the courtesy to express sympathy to a friend who has suffered a great loss. But with that mere expression of sympathy, that obligation fulfilled, do we have the understanding and the empathy to place ourselves in their position? Grief does not end at the graveside nor troubles disappear when someone says loudly, "If there is anything I can do just let me know." Where are our eyes? Where is our mind? Where is our sympathy? *Can I not see that sink full of dirty dishes, that floor that needs to be swept, that bed that needs to be made?*

If we are truly concerned, we will not only say but do what we can to be helpful and to prove our love. It is in times like these that our greatest, most lasting friendships are secured.

What we do not seem to consider is that those who need our kindness most will be the last to ask for it. Have you ever observed a friendly, sociable person suddenly pull into a shell, become unsociable, and go to noticeable lengths to avoid facing those he once trusted most? We can be certain this person has a deep problem which he is trying to carry alone. This is the time he needs most a friend and kind attention. Why does that old friend not come to you and ask for help and understanding? Perhaps pride is involved, but certainly there is a guard secured against being hurt by one who might let him down.

This being the case, it requires a great deal of courage on our part to go to that person and prove that we truly are concerned. It takes more than mere words; it takes time, effort and sacrifice. It takes a little hard work and a lot of caring but the rewards will never fail.

LOVE ENVIETH NOT

In this affluent nation we have been blessed with every enjoyable thing this world has to offer. Yet many of us have abused this privilege with selfishness and envy of those who have more than we do. A blessing becomes a curse if we cannot be content and thankful for what we have and make the most of it, or if we resent and begrudge others having nice things, being popular or influential. Envy is a product of hatred; so it is impossible to love someone and envy them at the same time. The only way to free one's self of envy and jealousy is through love.

Sometimes it appears that worldly people have more possessions, more fun, more talent and popularity than we do. But how much love, joy and peace of mind do these things bring? If we can have many of such things while seeking first the kingdom of heaven and its righteousness, then they are truly blessings from the Lord. But let us not deceive ourselves and become foolish to the point of putting our trust in fame, fortune and power. For these things are difficult to handle aright. Truth, honesty and self-reliance are more to be desired.

LOVE VAUNTETH NOT ITSELF: IS NOT PUFFED UP

Genuine love does not "put on airs, " or make a display of itself. Since love is from the heart it cannot be hypocritical but is pure and flows out to others freely and naturally.

A person can do a lot of talking about how much he loves the Lord and his fellowman. But his love is not true if his fruits are not of the spirit. If one's talk is self-centered and full of braggings, he thinks more highly of himself than he should.

A "puffed up" love seems to be a matter of false pride and uncer-

59

tainty, a means of convincing others one is really in good standing with the Lord—or with one's mate, or the church members, or anyone's love they are not sure of. This is a form of hypocritical love that will not sacrifice.

A meek and humble spirit displays love but does not parade itself. Humility has its rewards later—in wisdom, honor, riches and life. Jesus came to this earth in the form of a man. He humbled himself. He did not brag that he was the Son of God but proved his love by the things he suffered as a man: the injustices, outright cruelties and insults, the false accusations. He was crucified without complaint or personal protest and with a prayer that his Father forgive those who did not know what they were doing.

## DOTH NOT BEHAVE ITSELF UNSEEMLY

We are all sinners and we all do both good and evil, but if we diligently try, we can overcome evil with good. We are told to be strong in our convictions and have the courage to do what we know needs to be done.

Perhaps the greatest influence to our behavior pattern is the companions with whom we choose to spend our time. We must be alert to the dangers of becoming involved with evil or foolish companions. We soon will either become like them—deceitful and foolish—or will resort to cunning ways to avoid or appease them. If they become offended, there is not a thing they will not do to hurt us.

We must be alert and stay away from the person who has the false concept that she is being smart and wise by destroying a person she envies or wants to rise above. By devious means, whether she is aware of it or not, the self-deceiver may be out to win friends and get a following.

The scriptures have something to say about the person who is always ready to lend a listening ear to gossip, slander and scornful conversation. Naturally it takes time to get to know another person, what is in her heart and what her real motivation is. This being so, we should make it a point to never listen to a damaging remark about anyone. It is far better to walk away than to listen to anyone downgrading another person. God is not pleased with one who causes strife; neither is he pleased with one who lends a listening ear to those bent on confusion and strife. If one listens to the little critical opening remark of a talebearer, the stage is being set for a full rendition of character assassination.

If we use good judgment, we will not argue or debate with a person we already know will not listen. We would only be taking the chance of making a matter worse and making the gulf between us even wider. Often, a third person will come into an argument or disagreement for any number of reasons. If she becomes contentious, the difficulties are only beginning. So often we think we can be helpful by giving unwanted information or advice, undeserved sympathy or total devotion to the problems of others. (This is often the case if we are prone to be sympathetic with the "underdog.") But it is better to speak to listening ears than to those who will not hear.

A person is often taken in by flattery and deceived by her own need for attention and affection. Thus, she is drawn into unpleasant situations which are not her business. It is so easy to become innocently involved to our own hurt and destruction. Let us think seriously before we become involved by meddling in the affairs of others; realizing there may be involvements which do not concern us and which we could not understand.

Beware of those who are angry. Whether angry with God or with man, they seem to require someone to blame for all their faults, failures and problems.

For the good that one does she should be rewarded with praise from those who love her and who wish her well. These compliments add greatly to one's self-esteem, giving encouragement and motivation to do good always.

About the evil one does against you, you are told the first step is to go to the offender privately. It may be that he will listen, see his error and make it right and you will have gained a friend (Matthew 18:15).

If we repay evil with evil, we would stand to be condemned the same as the evil doer.

LOVE SEEKETH NOT HER OWN

A person who seeks everything for his own benefit or advantage is a selfish person; and selfishness is in no way a characteristic of love. It is always better to settle for simple necessities and be with those we love than to strive to become a millionaire and spend our time with the self-seeking worldly who have no concern for our wealth, only their own. "Better is a dinner of herbs where love is than a stalled ox and hatred therewith" (Proverbs 17:10).

We know this life is a pilgrimage and that God has promised to provide all the things we need if we put our complete trust in him (Matthew 6:31-33).

Like Paul, we must learn that happiness is not dependent upon the things we possess but on the inner qualities of the heart, the proper relationship with the Lord. While in prison, Paul penned these words,

"I have learned in whatsoever state I am therewith to be content" (Philippians 4:11). Paul's secret was in being able to lose all desire for things beyond his reach; to think on heavenly eternal things rather than earthly and temporal things. He learned to accept those things he could not change and to spend his time doing good, with a selfless devotion to God and man.

This is not to say that we should not try to improve our status in life, but that we must not put major emphasis on material things. After we have done all we can to improve our own condition and to help others, we are to contentedly leave all the consequences in God's hands.

We cannot deny that today's society rushes madly from place to place, from job to job, from meeting to meeting, in search of more fun and popularity, more power or more material possessions. The luxuries of life are greatly desired; but God's people must not overemphasize their importance. We must learn moderation and cultivate appreciation and contentment with the simple and necessary things of life.

# For Private Meditation
# Or Class Discussion

## LOVE GOD, SELF AND ONE ANOTHER

1. What is the first and great commandment? (Matthew 22:37).
2. What is the second great commandment given by Jesus? (Matthew 22:39).
3. How are we to love one another? "Seeing that ye love one another _____" (1 Peter 1:22b).
4. What does our love for one another show the world? (John 13:35).
5. What reward do we have if we do good only to those who love us? (Matthew 5:46-48).
6. All things work together for good for whom? (Romans 8:28).
7. What is the bond of perfection? (Colossians 3:14).
8. When do our good deeds for others profit us nothing? (1 Corinthians 13:1-3).

## LONGSUFFERING (1 Corinthians 13:4)

1. Why is God longsuffering with the evils of this world? (2 Peter 3:9).
2. Paul said that Jesus showed forth longsuffering to him for what reason? (1 Timothy 1:16).
3. Do you think the world is as evil as it was when God sent forth the flood? as the gentiles as Paul described them in Romans 1:21?
4. Do you know how much longer God will be longsuffering?
5. Discuss the lack of longsuffering in today's marriages and other relationships.
6. What did Paul advise us in 1 Thessalonians 5:14?
7. Blessings that come from being longsuffering:
   a. "I waited for the Lord and _____" (Psalms 40:1).
   b. "They that wait upon the Lord_____" (Isaiah 40:31).
   c. "In your patience ye shall _____" (Luke 21:19).
   d. "For we are made partakers of Christ, if _____" (Hebrews 3:14).

## KINDNESS (1 Corinthians 13:4)

1. What is kindness?

2. Paul gave these instructions: "Be ye _____" (Ephesians 4:32a).
3. Do you avoid a person who is always kind? Why not? "That which maketh a man _____" (Psalms 19:22a).
4. Although kindness extends to being helpful and giving of one's self, generally we are first won by it from what source?
   a. "A _____ is a tree of life" (Proverbs 15:14).
   b. "She openeth her mouth with wisdom; and ____" (Proverbs 31:26).
   c. "Let your speech be always _____ that ye may know how to answer each one" (Colossians 4:6).
5. Kindness requires a gentle, considerate nature or it will often be revealed as a sham. Sympathy and/or empathy should never be "for show." Is there a difference in sympathy and empathy?
6. How are we profited by the kindness we bestow?
   a. "A merciful man_____" (Proverbs 11:17a).
   b. "Whoso keepeth his mouth and his tongue _____" (Proverbs 21:23).

## LOVE VAUNTETH NOT ITSELF (1 Corinthians 13:4)

1. Since humility is the opposite of puffed up pride, how can we guard against being overly proud?
2. What precedes destruction and a fall according to Proverbs 16:18? "_____ goeth before destruction, and a _____ before a fall."

## DOTH NOT BEHAVE ITSELF UNSEEMLY (1 Corinthians 13:5)

1. A husband may be won over by his wife's good example of Christianity (1 Peter 3:1,2). Is this still true in spite of the fact it is considered very old-fashioned today?
   a. What is chaste behavior? "Denying ungodly and worldly lusts, ye should live _____ in this present world" (Titus 2:12).
   b. Why should we choose our companions carefully? "Evil companions _____" (1 Corinthians 15:33).
   c. Unseemly conduct is what?
2. Unseemly conduct is any behavior which is unbecoming to a Christian. This rebellion can be caused by any one of these personality flaws: pride, selfishness, envy, fear, self-pity or a guilty conscience.
   a. How can we avoid making evil companions? "A wise man __ from evil" (Proverbs 14:16a). "A prudent man _____ and

_____" (Proverbs 27:12).

   b. Results of choosing evil companions: "A companion of fools
_____" (Proverbs 13:20).

## STRIFE OF WORDS

1. Paul advised Timothy regarding one who uses strife of words in
doctrine (perverts the doctrine of Christ). He said, "From such
_____" (1 Timothy 6:4,5).
2. Contending with a foolish person—why not?
   a. "Speak not in the ears of a fool, for he will _____"
(Proverbs 23:9).
   b. "If a wise man contend with a foolish man, whether he rage
or laugh, _____" (Proverbs 29:9).
   c. "Go from the presence of a foolish man, when thou
perceivest not in him _____" (Proverbs 14:7).
   d. "One offended is harder to be won than _____ and
their contentions are like _____" (Proverbs 18:19).
3. Meddling:
   a. "Leave off contention_____; for this
is the beginning of strife" (Proverbs 17:4).
   b. "Meddle not with her _____" (Proverbs 20:19a).
   c. "Meddle not with them that _____: for their
calamity shall rise suddenly; and who knoweth the ruin of
them both" (Proverbs 24:21,22).
4. Lying and slander:
   a. "He that hideth hatred _____, and he that
_____ is a fool" (Proverbs 10:18).
   b. "A wicked doer giveth heed to _____" (Proverbs 17:4a).
5. Anger:
"Make no friendship with _____; and with a furious
man thou _____ lest thou learn his ways and get
_____" (Proverbs 22:24).
6. Vengeance:
   a. Are we to repay evil for evil?
"Recompense to no man _____" (Romans 12:17a).
   b. Who will repay a man for the evil he has done?
"Dearly beloved, _____, but rather give place
unto wrath; for it is written, " 'I will repay, saith the Lord' "
(Romans 12:19).
   c. Is God unrighteous who taketh vengeance?
"God forbid: for then how shall God____?" (Romans 3:5,6).

LOVE SEEKETH NOT HER OWN (1 Corinthians 13:5)

1. If we spend our lifetime trying to get ahead of everyone in everything, what will we have in the end? "For we brought...and it is for certain _____" (1 Timothy 6:7).
2. Since we are to work for a living, the Lord expects us to do the best we can—for what persons?
   a. "If any _____" (2 Thessalonians 3:10b).
   b. "With quietness they _____" (2 Thessalonians 3:12b).
   c. "Not _____, fervent in spirit, serving _____" (Romans 12:11).
   d. "Let him that stole_____: but rather let him labor, _____ the thing which is good, that he may have to _____" (Ephesians 4:28).

66

## Chapter Nine

# Love God, Self and One Another Continued

## LOVE IS NOT EASILY PROVOKED

Love is tolerant and is not easily irritated nor offended. It is not easy to be tolerant and to accept peacefully the things we cannot change in the midst of violence and broken vows and promises. Because of the frustrations caused by social injustices, there is a vast impulse/trend to turn inward for self-preservation. This impulse causes one to forget everything and everybody except "me and my own."

Our modern therapists are geared to helping people keep from becoming exiles to this kind of privation. Even certain religious groups of our day stress entirely, "What can I do for myself?" rather than, "What can I do to help all people?" Christianity has proved that happiness comes from involvements with other people. This requires strong personal commitments which cannot be easily provoked and the ability to sacrifice for others.

There are things which can provoke us to the extent of discouragement and anger. It requires a lot of love and self-control to keep from getting annoyed, impatient and angry when someone or something is aggravating us to the point of irritation or anger.

There are many things which can be provoking in our daily walk of life. At times, our closest ties and relationships become a strain. We can spend too much time together, become too intimate and too involved to withstand the test of overlooking and enduring all those little things which can become so annoying. What close friends do not at times spend too much time together? What mother does not come to the point of irritation with her little children when it seems she is nothing but a full-time slave to them? If her reactions are not kind and gentle, even in firm discipline, she will cause a vicious circle by provoking her children. What couple does not get on each other's nerves, becoming discouraged at times? If their love is strong enough they will not be provoked and go around with a "chip on their shoulder." Rather they should be flexible enough to roll with the punches, using those very differences to enrich their relationship.

## LOVE THINKETH NO EVIL

A woman's thoughts are the tools by which she makes and shapes her own character and destiny. She may fashion her thoughts intelligently, patiently and ceaselessly until she comes to an understanding of herself. Or, she may neglect to cultivate the habit of pure thinking. Whether her thoughts are cultivated and controlled or are allowed to run wild, they will bring forth of the seed that was sown. Just as a woman tends her garden, keeping it free from weeds, cultivating, feeding and watering, it continues to grow and bring forth good fruits, in like manner she tends the garden of her mind. Every thought, whether good or evil, produces of its own kind. Good thoughts bear good fruit, evil thoughts bear bad fruit. A person with pure thoughts will not suddenly become a criminal. But a man of evil thoughts will reveal his own evil impurities.

A woman and prayers are answered in harmony with her thoughts and actions. A woman cannot improve her way of life until she improves herself. If she is miserably poor and desires to be rich yet will not work, she is deceiving herself with impossible thoughts. Pure thoughts and actions can never produce bad results. Evil thoughts and actions can never produce good results.

Material possessions are not a measure of our thinking, but, if wisely and unselfishly used, riches are a blessing. Otherwise a woman can be rich and cursed solely because of her riches.

A person builds herself up with fine and noble thoughts and regulates her life, ceasing to whine, complain and blame others for her failures. Then she discovers the "hidden powers" and possibilities which she possesses. With justice and righteousness she finds that by altering her thoughts toward other people, other people will alter their thoughts toward her. Thoughts cannot be kept secret—thoughts evolve into habits and habits into circumstances. Evil thoughts bring forth fears, doubts, suspicions, indecision; and these evolve into circumstances which end in failure, dependence, dishonesty, violence and injury. Selfish thoughts lead to self-seeking whereas beautiful thoughts form habits of kindness, gentleness, moderation, self control and peace of mind. Our thoughts are ever moving—let us keep them pure. Let us think well of all, be kind to all, look for the good in all; and our thoughts of peace toward others will bring peace to us.

## LOVE REJOICES NOT IN INIQUITY BUT IN THE TRUTH

The unchristian world around us rejoices in unspiritual instincts, appetites and moral poverty. Many mistrust and dislike the self-denying love and obedience which God demands of his children. It is this love which helps God's children to be trusting, pure, obedient, patient and strong. The spirit of worldliness is the spirit of love for those things which minister to the lusts of men rather than to the love of God and his truths.

Bodily appetites are not wrong within themselves but when the Spirit of love for God, neighbor and self ceases to dwell in the body, it becomes corrupt and asserts itself in sensuality.

The "lust of the flesh" is a starving soul deprived of healthy nutrition. The "lust of the eye" is covetous—for the satisfying of which *sight* is the tool. We see and we want all the luxuries of the world. The "pride of life" is the desire for power and fame. The pursuit of worldly knowledge, science and art, apart from the spiritual needs of life, become the object of men's devotion.

We must be alert to the dangers of becoming gradually influenced by the evils of this world. Little by little these influences can blind us to the truth. God's children do not court the intimacy of the unchristian world, nor keep company with it. Although the worldly people are in the majority, they have nothing lasting to give. At the time it may seem joyous to walk with them but they cannot contribute to a joyful hope of a better life beyond. "Know ye not that the friendship of the world is enmity with God?" (James 4:4).

We cannot reject the truths which are upsetting to us for the things which coincide with our whims and desires. We cannot convert the world by becoming like it. Instead, the world will convert us to the idealogy that gives Christ a place in history but does not accept his teachings concerning himself and the Church. The wisdom "of this world" cannot conform to the word of God. The spirit which makes this planet into *the world* is not a friend, but an enemy of God. We are neither to love, imitate, nor rejoice with this spirit.

The truth is, our joy comes from communion with Christ and his righteousness. The light of his love and the comfort of his presence gives us confidence and strength. If our hearts dwell on Christ and his wondrous love, his spirit will flow out to others.

69

## LOVE BEARETH ALL THINGS

When our love is strong for God and mankind we can bear the ordeals which try our patience. We can love the unlovable. When we "put up with" the imperfections in ourselves and in others we become understanding and flexible, able to adjust to all situations and circumstances.

It is not easy to bear with changing social conditions when our daily jobs take us into a quagmire of worldliness. But we must live in this world. At the same time, we must not be like the world.

All relationships require a lot of overlooking and a lot of "putting up with" things that irritate us. Proper value judgments are essential qualities. Some of these qualities are: courtesy, humility, honesty, sincerity, and spiritual wisdom.

If our love for the Lord is strong, we can bear up under the worst personal losses—even the loss of a loved one, health, material wealth, security or friends. Remember, God has promised that he will always be with us. Even in the midst of fears, anxieties and worries, we can bear them with God's help. We can keep on believing, hoping and loving.

## LOVE BELIEVETH ALL THINGS

Are you eager to believe the truth? All people are guided by things which they believe. In this way our characters are formed by the things we believe. Likewise, our ability to cope creatively with the troubled areas of our lives is formed on our beliefs. Although we all have troubles in this world, there is a way we can handle these problems. Walking in the footsteps of Jesus is the solution. Jesus said, "In the world ye shall have tribulation; but be of good cheer; I have overcome the world" (John 16:33).

We have needs and the love of God has furnished all the answers to our needs if we but use God's answers. We believe we need a Savior, someone who loves us and will safely direct our footsteps throughout this lifetime. On the cross, Jesus Christ took on himself the complete responsibility of doing this for the entire human race. The greatest tragedy of all is when Jesus' followers refuse to let him act on the responsibility he has assumed.

Have we really faced our own need of a Savior? Do we love and believe him enough that we can have the spirit of Christ dwelling in us? Do we believe that God blesses us according to our merits? or does he bless us because of his love and mercy and grace? If we believe our blessings and salvation are based on merits, we would be compelled to ask, "Then why did he not protect his own Son from the cross?" Certainly his sinless life did not merit such torture and death!

Our faith comes from learning, believing and understanding how much God really loves us. After we have set our course on the path of righteousness, God's love gives us the confidence needed to trust his guidance in each particular circumstance of our lives. God is love and God cannot lie. These facts give us assurance we can trust every word God has given us. Now if our love for each other is patterned after his love for us, we can never doubt each other's truthfulness. Neither can we lie or deceive one another.

## LOVE HOPETH ALL THINGS

We are in God's family by having obeyed that "form of doctrine" which Paul explains in Romans 6:3,11,18. Romans 6:12 concludes, "Let not sin therefore remain in your mortal body, that ye should obey it in the lusts thereof." Romans 6:22 continues, "But now being made free from sin and become servants of God, ye have your fruit unto holiness and the end everlasting life."

By living one day at a time, we can put up with the annoyances of each day as we continue toward our goal, believing in and hoping for a brighter new tomorrow.

Only through knowledge of the word of God can we have hope. The more we learn of God, the more we love him. Our love for mankind increases our trust in God's loving care for us and our hope in his promises of a peaceful life and an eternal inheritance.

Hope expresses itself in patience; patience assures endurance. The Lord has promised to be our director all the way. Our need for hope becomes a reality. This hope purifies a man and makes life worth living (1 John 3:3).

In times of trouble, trials, worries and grief, we often feel all is vain and hopeless. Yet, with God's help and his promise that he will not let us be faced with more than we can bear, that he will protect and strengthen our hope—we will cling to our faith, guard our love and retain our hope (Isaiah 40:31).

Let us remember: *Small things are important; they add up to a full life and a life full of hope.*

## LOVE ENDURETH ALL THINGS

Since God is love—and he loves us so much he sacrificed his only begotten son that we might receive the gift of eternity—he made it possible for us to adjust our lives to his will and to endure all hard-

71

ships. God promised us that we would not be tried beyond our endurance (1 Corinthians 10:13).

Does God punish us by affliction to prove how much we can endure? I think not. It is his love and longsuffering which gives us sufficient time to be led to repentance, to be forgiven and thus strengthened to endure affliction.

When Jesus was on trial and Peters' endurance was at low ebb, three times Peter denied that he knew Jesus. Then Jesus looked at him. Peter remembered the Lord had predicted this would happen. His heart was broken when he remembered Jesus' warning and love for him so he went out and wept bitterly (Matthew 26:75). This must have been one of the most severe punishments of Peter's life. Yet he rose above his lack of faith and became one of the greatest teachers of all time (Luke 22:31).

We have the examples of so many faithful followers of the Lord who endured unbelievable hardships. Abraham left his home with all he had to be led by God to a better place. He suffered hardships and his faith was tried to the extreme when God told him to offer his son as a sacrifice. Although God did not permit him to commit the act, it was "a like figure" of God's sacrifice of his only son (Hebrews 11:8,19).

Moses, by faith, chose to suffer affliction with the people of God rather than to enjoy the pleasures of sin for a time as the son of Pharaoh's daughter. He forsook Egypt, for he endured, as seeing him who is invisible (Hebrews 11:29).

Kings and prophets and faithful followers of the true and living God endured unbelievable hardships believing they would receive a better reward. They "quenched the violence of fire, escaped the edge of the sword, out of weakness were made strong, waxed valiant in fight, turned to flight the armies of the aliens." And "others had trial of cruel mockings and scourgings; yea, moreover of bonds and imprisonment: they were stoned, they were sawn asunder, were tempted, were slain with the sword; they wandered about in sheepskins and goatskins; being destitute, afflicted, tormented, they wandered in deserts, and in mountains, and in dens and caves of the earth. And these all having obtained a good report through faith, received not the promise; God having provided some better thing for us, that they without us should not be made perfect" (Hebrews 11:37-40).

Then Jesus came to earth as a man, lived a sinless life and became a willing sacrifice for our sins and theirs. He paid the price of forgiveness for us and for those faithful followers of God in former ages. His death, which made possible the forgiveness of our sins and perfecting of our love, made it also possible for those followers of ancient times, who endured to the end of their lives, to be perfected in the love of God and the Lord and Savior Jesus Christ.

## LOVE NEVER FAILS

God is love. When we accept and understand this biblical fact, we know that worldly love which leaves God out is not love at all but selfishness and lust.

Love is the one power within our human experience which reveals and reflects what is real and abiding. Only with this power can we do the will of God. Knowing that God loves us, that he forgives and forgets our sins, that he sent Jesus into the world to save sinners, makes it possible for the scriptures to be functional in our daily lives.

If we love God, we will put our trust in his power to guide us in the way that is best for us. We will look to him as a loving child looks to his earthly father for his needs and his guidance and protection. A loving father never fails to do what he thinks is best for his children. How much more concern we can expect from our heavenly Father! He loves us. He will never let us down. Neither will he let us go. These things we do to ourselves (Matthew 7:9-11).

There is no more positive statement in all the scriptures than that spoken by Jesus, "If you love me you will keep my commandments" (John 14:15,23). How can so many people be so unconcerned about searching for themselves the commandments of God? How can they fail to believe there is no higher power than themselves? How do they dare "do their own thing"? How can they go through a lifetime not learning that they cannot direct their own footsteps? These things are hard for us to understand because we know that God's love has never failed us. They are hard to understand because our own love for God and for all mankind has made life bearable in spite of trials and sufferings—we can live in peace and contentment with a good conscience before God and man.

# For Private Meditation
# Or Class Discussion

LOVE IS NOT EASILY PROVOKED (1 Corinthians 13:5)

1. Can God be provoked? (Psalms 78:37-42).
2. How did God deal with the Israelites when they disobeyed and provoked him? (Psalms 78:56-62; Romans 10:19-21).
3. How can fathers discourage their children? (Colossians 3:21).
4. How are fathers to correct and punish their children? (Ephesians 6:4).
5. Is there love in a marriage where there is bitterness? (Colossians 3:19).
6. How many marriages would fail if they were based on the kind of love described in 1 Corinthians 13:4-7?

LOVE THINKETH NO EVIL (1 Corinthians 13:5)

1. Can a person dwell on evil thoughts without them showing in her character and actions? (Proverbs 23:7a).
2. Who cleanses our heart and gives us a pure conscience and a new start? "Who can say I have made my _____?" (Proverbs 20:9). "I thought on my ways, and _____" (Psalms 115:59).
3. Paul told us to think on these things: "Finally, brethren, whatsoever things are_____, whatsoever things are_____, whatsoever things are_____, whatsoever things are_____, whatsoever things are_____, whatsoever things are of_____, if there be any virtue, and if there be any praise, think on these things (Philippians 4:8).
4. "Keep thy heart_____; for out of it are the issues of life" (Proverbs 4:23).

LOVE REJOICES IN TRUTH (1 Corinthians 13:6)

1. What is truth and what does it do for us?
   a. "_____ is truth" (John 17:17).
   b. "Ye shall know the truth, and the truth shall _____" (John 8:32).
   c. When Thomas questioned Jesus, he answered, "I am the _____, and the life; no man cometh unto the Father _____" (John 14:6).

74

2. What does the Lord love and care for?
   a. "The Lord loves _____" (Isaiah 61:8).
   b. "The Lord loves_____" (Micah 6:8).
   c. "God commended _____, in that while we were yet sinners, Christ died for us" (Romans 5:8).
   d. "The eyes of the Lord are _____ and his ears are open _____; but the face of the Lord is against them that do evil" (1 Peter 3:12).
3. What does the Lord command us to love and to hate?
   a. "Ye that love the Lord, _____" (Psalms 97:10).
   b. "Hate evil and _____" (Amos 5:15).
   c. "Love not the world, neither _____" (1 John 2:15).
   d. "Therefore, love_____" (Zechariah 8:19b).
4. What can keep us from rejoicing in the truth? Why is it true that worldly people hate the word of God more than anything else?
   a. "...because _____" (John 3:18-21; especially verse 19).
   b. "Vainly puffed up by his _____ mind" (Colossians 2:18).
5. Application:
   a. Can we rejoice in both truth and evil at the same time?
   b. Why can we not be on both sides (or on neither side) and keep ourselves from getting involved? (Matthew 6:24).
   c. How can we always be on the side of truth?
      (1). "And __and the truth shall make you free" (John 8:32).
      (2). "What five things does James tell us to do to remain on truth's side? (James 4:7,8,10).
   d. How are we to love each other?
      (1). "With a pure heart _____" (1 Peter 1:22).
      (2). "Speak not____ one of another, brethren" (James 4:11).
   e. What should we feel in the love of each other? (Philemon 7; Philippians 2:3,4).
   f. How can I rejoice in myself? (Galatians 6:14).
   g. What is the fate of those who rejoice in iniquity? (Proverbs 8:36; 12:2b).

LOVE BEARETH ALL THINGS (1 Corinthians 13:7)

1. Why can Christians bear anything through the love we possess? (1 John 4:18; 2 Timothy 1:7; 1 Corinthians 13:4).
2. Why did our parents "bear with" our attitudes and behavior as we were growing up?
3. How do we "put up with" the protests and stubbornness of our children? How do we best deal with this?

75

4. How does my husband and children bear with my faults and weaknesses?
5. When trying to teach others of Christ, why must I exercise patience and understanding, yet have the courage to present the truth and not give up easily? (2 Timothy 2:24,26).
6. Which is easier to bear—being accused of a sin of which you are guilty or of one which you are innocent?
   a. If guilty, how should you handle it? (Acts 8:22).
   b. If innocent, how should you handle it? How did Jesus, our example, bear false accusations? (1 Peter 2:21,23).

LOVE BELIEVETH ALL THINGS (1 Corinthians 13:7)

Let us discuss some of the things which we believe are essential to living a life that is full of love and pleasing to God; a life that will secure our inheritance of eternal life with God.
1. Concerning seeking God, we believe:
   a. "God is; and that he is a rewarder of them that _____" (Hebrews 11:6b).
   b. "Seek _____" (Matthew 7:7b).
   c. "If _____, God dwells in us, and his love is __." "The Father sent the Son to be __." "Whosoever __, God dwelleth in him and he in God." "God is love; God loves us, and he that dwelleth _____" (1 John 4:12,14-16).
2. Concerning obedience, we believe:
   a. "We ought to obey God, _____" (Acts 5:29).
   b. "God heareth not sinners; but if any man be a _____ _____, him he heareth" (John 9:31).
   c. "God is a spirit, and they that worship him _____" (John 4:24).
   d. "Thy_____ is truth" (John 17:17).
   e. "Hereby know we that we dwell in him and he in us because _____" (1 John 4:13).
   f. "Repent and be baptized _____ in the name of Jesus Christ for the remission of sins and ye shall receive _____ (Acts 2:38).
3. Concerning mercy, we believe:
   a. We must be merciful and forgiving.
      (1). "Be ye kind one to another, tenderhearted, _____ even as God for Christ's sake hath forgiven you" (Ephesians 4:32).
      (2). "When ye stand praying, forgive _____: that your Father also, which is in heaven, may forgive you your

trespasses; but if you do not forgive _____ which is in heaven _____" (Mark 11:25,26).

b. On forgiving:
   (1). How do we know if we have really forgiven others?
   (2). What is the meaning of "tenderhearted" as used in Ephesians 4:32 (KJV)? Does it have reference to one's self— of being easily offended, or does it have reference to the mercy, compassion and understanding we are to extend to others?
   (3). If another Christian offends you, is it difficult to be friends again? Why is this so? How does Proverbs 12:19 relate?
   (4). What is the first thing Jesus has told us to do if someone has hurt our feelings? (Matthew 18:15,16). How does Philippians 2:4 relate?
       If both hearts are loving, the outcome will always be happy and rewarding. Great is Jesus' example for us! Even while dying on the cross he prayed, "Father, forgive them; for they know not what they do."

c. We must be humble and patient.
   (1). "He hath showed thee, O man, what is good and what doth the Lord require of thee, but to _____and to _____ and to _____ with thy God" (Micah 6:8).
   (2). "Humble yourselves therefore under the mighty hand of God, that he may _____" (1 Peter 5:6).
   (3). "Let us lay aside every weight and the sin which doth so easily beset us, and let us _____ that is set before us" (Hebrews 12:1b).

d. We must do good to all mankind.
   (1). "See thou none render evil for evil unto any man; but ever follow that which is good _____" (Ephesians 5:15).
   (2). "As we have therefore opportunity, let us do good unto all men, _____" (Galatians 6:10).

4. Concerning following Jesus, we believe:
   "Then Jesus said unto his disciples, 'If any man will come after me, let him deny himself and take up his cross and follow me. For the Son of Man shall come in the glory of his Father with his angels and then he shall reward every man_____" (Matthew 16:24,27).

THE HOPE OF LOVE (1 Corinthians 13:7)

1. How do we learn to have hope?

a. "...but I hope _____" (Psalms 119:81b).
b. "...that we through_____might have hope" (Romans 15:4b).
2. In whom do we put our hope?
a. "_____ which is our hope" (1 Timothy 1:1b).
3. What should we hope for?
a. "In hope of _____" (Titus 1:2).
b. "Looking for that blessed hope, and the_____
_____" (Titus 2:13).
c. "For the hope which is laid up for you_____
_____" (Colossians 1:5).
d. "And hope toward God...that there shall be a _____
both of the just and the unjust" (Acts 24:15).
4. How do we lay hold on that hope, and how do we hold onto it?
a. "But let us who are of the day, be sober,_____
and for an helmet _____" (1 Thessalonians 5:8).
b. "And we desire that every one of you do show this same diligence to the _____ unto the end" (Hebrews 6:11).

## LOVE ENDURETH ALL THINGS (1 Corinthians 13:7)

1. Why has God endured the sinfulness of this world so many centuries?
a. "The Lord is not slack concerning his promise, but is longsuffering to usward, _____, but that all should come to repentance" (2 Peter 3:9).
b. "Account that the longsuffering of our Lord _____" (2 Peter 3:15a).
2. Why does God care if we are saved or lost? "For God _____ that _____, that whosoever believeth in him should not perish but have everlasting life" (John 3:16).
3. What can we always be assured of as our guide? "____ endureth forever" (1 Peter 1:25).
4. In the previous studies, we mentioned some things that we believe because of our love for God, Jesus and his righteousness. Among those assets are: we must be merciful and forgiving and humble and patient; and we mut do good to all mankind. With love, we have the courage to become bold and to perfect our love. How is this possible? "There is no fear in love, but _____ because hath torment. He that feareth is not made perfect in love" (1 John 4:18).
5. Since no one is sinless, how is it possible for us to endure to the

end? "Though he fall, he shall not be utterly cast down: for____.
For the Lord loveth judgment, and _____; they are preserved
forever" (Psalms 37:24,28).

6. Can we remain saints unconditionally? "Then said Jesus to
those Jews which believed on him, ' _____, then are ye my
disciples indeed' " (John 8:31).

7. Can anything separate us from the love of God? Paul wrote to
the saints at Rome, "For I am persuaded that ____, _____
life, _____ principalities, _____ powers, _____
things present, _____ things to come, _____height,
_____ depth, _____ any other creature, _____,
which is in Christ Jesus our Lord" (Romans 8:38,39).

LOVE NEVER FAILS (1 Corinthians 13:8)

1. What is love? "_____ is love" (1 John 4:8).
2. How can we make use of this love? "This is love, that we ____"
   (2 John 6a).
3. If we walk after his commandments we can be assured of what?
   "He that dwelleth in love, dwelleth in God, ____" (1 John 4:16).
4. Love never fails because it gives us the *security of belonging.*
   Jesus said to the apostles, "_____" (John 15:16).
5. Love never fails because it gives us a *sense of direction.*
   a. Jesus said, "I am _____; no man cometh to the Father
      but by me" (John 14:6).
   b. Jesus said, "I am the_____" (John 14:9).
   c. Jesus said, "I am the _____" (John 14:11).
6. Love never fails because *it gives us guidance.* "...the name of
   _____ neither is there salvation in any other; for there is
   _____ under heaven given among man, _____"
   (Acts 4:10b,12).
7. Circumstances need not determine the kind of life we live. "I can
   do all things _____ which strengtheneth me" (Philippians 4:13).
8. God rewards those whose love never fails.
   a. "God is our refuge and strength, _____"
      (Psalms 46:1).
   b. "The Lord shall preserve thee_____"; "He shall
      _____" (Psalms 121:7).
   c. "The Lord preserveth all them _____: but all the wicked
      will he destroy" (Psalms 145:20).
   d. Great peace have they _____ and they have no
      occasion for stumbling" (Psalms 119:165).

79

e. "Who is he that overcometh the world, but _____?" (1 John 5:5).

f. "But thanks be to God, which giveth us the victory through _____" (1 Corinthians 15:57).

9. Why are there so many failures today in marriage and family ties? in business? in political dealings? in love? in faithfulness to the church?

## Chapter Ten
# When Strife Ceases—Peace Prevails

Peace prevails in our hearts when we have become spiritually mature. This means we have learned to be objective in our thinking patterns, especially in difficult, worrisome situations which we cannot escape. We have learned the causes of strife, to flee from them whenever possible. We must earnestly strive to live with a peaceful mind in all circumstances.

Once our thoughts are directed toward doing the will of God as our first purpose in life, we are on the way to achieving peace, joy and happiness. Without this first purpose, we are weakened by doubts, fears and self-pity. All changes begin with the particular change of a particular heart. Characters grow to find contentment and peace of mind.

It takes real effort and steadfastness to achieve any objective. There will be trials, struggles and failures along the way. These all add up to experience which is essential before we can overcome all obstacles.

Peace of mind is given by God along with wisdom. A person who has it has come to accept people and things as they are. That person understands and controls herself and adapts herself to others who in turn respect her spiritual strength. Others feel she is one who can be relied upon. She has replaced worries, doubts and fears with poise and serenity.

Peace of mind is the last lesson of the fruit bearing season. It is a poised, purified, well-balanced, self-controlled, and powerful way of life. Peace of mind is the outstanding characteristic of the mature Christian and her good spiritual health.

With God's help, we have learned to be patient, wise and understanding as were both David and his son Solomon. They were given wisdom from above after they searched and learned God's ways, acquiring patience, self-control, faith, hope and love.

God, at times, has turned evil around to accomplish good as in the case of Joseph and his brothers. Through envy, Joseph's brothers sold him as a slave, then set about to deceive their father into believing that he was dead. Can we even begin to imagine what went on in the minds of his brothers prior to the famine that forced them to go to Egypt to buy food? In Egypt, these same brothers saw Joseph and remembered what they had done to him and his father, Jacob. In fulfillment of Joseph's childhood dreams, they bowed down to him and said, "Behold we be thy servants." Joseph's answer was "Fear not, for am I in the place of God?" They feared his vengeance but he assured them God had used their evil to accomplish good (Genesis 37:1-36; 50:18-20).

## IDENTIFYING OUR PROBLEMS

It is so easy to be happy and at peace with ourselves when we feel a strong bond of love with everyone and when we are in excellent health. Our joy and optimism is at a high level when all is going well. But, when everyone and everything seems to be going against us, it is very difficult to keep from hitting the depth of despair.

During these times, we must evaluate and categorize our troubles. We should ask ourselves what has caused our problems and what can we do about them. First, we must examine ourselves. Perhaps something we have done or said may be pricking our conscience and plaguing our peace of mind. Then, it is self that needs to be changed and the situation will disappear. Secondly, we must honestly face the possibility that the situation may be our wounded pride and hurt feelings, that we have more ego than we should have. In this case, we often magnify a trifle far beyond its importance. We must examine the possibility of being guilty of envy, judging others, being filled with fear and doubts. If this is the case, these things will hound us and destroy our faith.

Are we sick, lonely, fatigued, prejudiced, our nerves on raw edge because we have taken on too much or too many responsibilities? Many fears are born of these distresses.

## CAN THIS SITUATION BE CHANGED AND SHOULD IT BE?

After we have decided a situation should be changed and are deciding how best to go about it, we will be mustering the courage to follow through. We must take care to make things better instead of worse; to gain love and peace rather than anger, hate and hostility. This requires the very best use of our Christian characters. Let us be very careful in judging others, remembering that Jesus was accused many times when he was not guilty.

## IF A SITUATION CANNOT BE CHANGED

When we have decided we would be stirring up strife if we tried to change a situation or a person, then we must face facts, accept it as something we cannot change and live peaceably with this knowledge. It is useless to worry over things of the past which cannot be changed. It is fruitless to worry over a present situation we cannot change. We must control our anxiety and change our thinking. We must realize that self-pity is a waste of time and utterly useless. Prayer and trusting in the Lord helps us accept the things and people which cannot be changed. We must accept it peaceably and go on living above reproach, realizing the problem is not ours to solve.

## THE WISDOM TO KNOW THE DIFFERENCE

The first consideration is to determine how important the problem is. Will the outcome affect the salvation of our soul or the other soul involved? If it will, then our concern is justified. If not, we are magnifying its importance and should accept and live with it peacefully.

One of the most important attributes of an individual is the ability to get along well with others. A good heart desires peace above all things. However, peace is not always possible. Paul wrote the church at Rome, "If it is possible, as much as lieth within you, live peacefully with all men" (Romans 12:18). God gives us the only basis for peace among all men: "Let us walk by the same rule" (Philippians 3:16). This infallible rule, by the authority of God, is the word of God, the Bible.

## SOLVING OUR PROBLEMS

God wants us to cry out to him in our troubles, whatever they may be. God knows our weaknesses and our capacities and how to deal with them. He knows what is best for our immediate and eternal welfare. Even if his response to our prayers seems at times to be negative, we still know that he knows what is best for us. If we ask God, in simple faith, to help us carry our burdens, to solve our problems, and to give us peace, he will do so. Our fears will be destroyed when we learn to love and trust God as much as he loves us. We must ask God believing that he will answer our prayers.

Many times we have known Christians who have continued to be plagued with the guilt of a particular sin and carried the heavy burden on their shoulders for many years to come, even after having repented and asked God and the brethren to forgive. Either these people lack understanding of God's promise (his very purpose for coming to earth as a man) or they just do not believe that when we repent, God does forgive our sins. Surely, if God and our brethren can forgive us, we should be able to forgive ourselves. God has given us this magnificent, mysterious gift. What a joy and a blessing to unload the burden and cast all our cares upon the Lord; for he cares for us.

If we keep constant company with our failures and dwell on them we are not going to make progress toward a successful life. Fear robs us of our faith. *God has forgotten our failure, why can't we?* Failure can serve no purpose except to be a yoke around our neck and a hindrance to progress.

If we compare ourselves with and strive to be as physically successful as others, we are following the wrong example. Jesus is the perfect example we have and we can learn of him through the word and by those who imitate Jesus. The course to follow is to do the best we can with what we have and to continually learn and strive to be superior to our previous selves.

Each day we can grow more Christ-like. Each day we should try to become more righteous, show more patience and persistence, be more forgiving, kind and loving. Thus we gain more peace of mind and the ability to accept things that cannot be changed with more tranquility and to live with a greater peace of mind.

"Let us therefore follow after the things which make for peace and things wherewith one may edify another" (Romans 14:19).

Jesus, our perfect example, was acquainted with all the sorrow, grief, hurts and pain we can ever experience. He opened his heart to all the woes of man. In spite of the things he suffered, his spirit was never crushed. He lived in peace and serenity and wherever he went, he carried rest, peace, joy and gladness.

Each day that his love reigns in our hearts, we shall follow his example. We will imitate his earnestness of purpose and his deep sense of personal responsibility.

When our ways have become pleasing to the Lord, no man can prevail against our spiritual welfare. We manifest a maturity of the Spirit through love that has been longsuffering and strengthened by the endurance of hardships and trials. Our tempers will be softened and our anger controlled. Our envy will be replaced by joy in the good fortune of others. Our pride will be in the Lord rather than ourselves. Our tongue will be self-contained—trained to avoid gossip, talebearing, meddling and mischief. All temptations will be overcome by taking advantage of God's way of escape. In dealing with others, we will grant them also time to grow.

Our ultimate purpose is to center our life in Christ as our Savior and our Life. We who are not sinless have shown our faith in letting Christ act like himself through us. Jesus hates the hypocrisy of those who try to imitate the seemingly good. Christ is our example, and in him we put our trust. God helps us see ourselves as we really are—we will not be pleased, nevertheless, such an insight will make us more tolerant and bring us to a realization of our constant dependence upon God.

"Now the God of hope fill you with all joy and peace in believing, that ye may abound in hope, through the power of the Holy Spirit" (Romans 15:13).

Because God is merciful and full of grace, we place our hope in him and in the Lord Jesus Christ. (1 Timothy 1:1). We place our hope in God's word which gives us patience and comfort (Romans 15:4). Our hope is found in the word of God. The scriptures show us the way to patience and comfort. In God and in Jesus Christ, is our hope. Our hope of salvation is like a protective helmet. It is an anchor to the soul both sure and steadfast (Hebrews 6:19). Our hope should endure with full assurance to the end (Hebrews 6:11).

## ASPECTS OF OUR HOPE

1. To know why he called us and to know the riches of the glory of his inheritance (Ephesians 1:18).
2. We are called in one hope toward God, given eternal life based on a resurrection of the dead (Colossians 1).
3. "The hope which is laid up for you in heaven" (Colossians 1:5).
4. God promised it before the world began" (Titus 1:2).
5. "We, having a living hope by the resurrection of Jesus Christ from the dead..." (1 Peter 1:3).
6. "The glorious appearing of God and our Lord and Saviour Jesus Christ..." (Titus 2:13).
7. "For the grace to be brought unto you at the revelation of Jesus Christ..." (1 Peter 1:13).
8. "There shall be a resurrection of the dead, both of the just and unjust" (Acts 24:15).
9. "Blessed is the man that trusteth in the Lord and whose hope the Lord is" (Jeremiah 17:7).
10. "Rejoicing in hope; patient in tribulation; continuing steadfastly in prayer" (Romans 12:12).

In the uncertainties of this life, we must not lose hope. Our attention should be on the realities of life, the certainty of death, and our hope in the resurrection of Jesus Christ. These are the things that deepen our confidence and give us joy and peace of mind.

Peace from strife is a matter of the heart's condition. Our aim and purpose has been to eliminate the problems that make it impossible to have peace of mind and get along peaceably with others.

When we cannot change a matter or a person because of someone's selfish, stubborn attitude, and when we have accepted this situation serenely, we have ceased from strife. At this point we realize the problem is not ours—it is the problem of the one who causes the problem. When we have reached this point, we will take great joy in realizing the great growth we have experienced in strength of character and Christian maturity.

## PEACE OF MIND THROUGH GOD AND HIS SON JESUS CHRIST

Christ is the Prince of Peace: "Of the increase of his government and peace there shall be no end" (Isaiah 9:7b).

Toward the end of his life Jesus had convinced his disciples that he was from God and would soon depart this world to return to heaven to rule as King. He told his disciples, "These things I have spoken unto you, that in me ye might have peace. In the world ye shall have tribulations; but be of good cheer: I have overcome the world" (John 16:33).

The glad tidings of good things preached in the gospel is called "The Gospel of Peace" (Ephesians 6:15).

Paul wrote the Philippians, "In nothing be anxious; but in everything by prayer and supplication with thanksgiving, let your requests be made known unto God. And the peace of God which passeth all understanding shall keep your hearts and minds through Christ Jesus" (Philippians 4:6,7).

This peace from God is deep within the hearts of his children. One of the last promises Jesus made his disciples was, "Peace I leave with you, my peace I give unto you: not as the world giveth, give I you. Let not your hearts be troubled, neither let them be afraid" (John 14:27).

To the Thessalonian church, Paul wrote, "Now the Lord of Peace himself give you peace, always by all means. The Lord be with you all" (2 Thessalonians 3:16).

Peace is bestowed upon us continually, as soothing as a gentle flowing river—not here today and gone tomorrow. It is a gift of God the Father and the Lord Jesus Christ.

The most effective conclusion for these lessons is to be found in the words of a song we often sing in worship services, a song in which is to be found the greatest "spiritual lift" when one is alone and in need of a spiritual uplift.

"Whatever my lot, Thou hast taught me to say,
It is well, it is well with my soul."

# For Private Meditation
# Or Class Discussion

ESSENTIALS TO PEACE OF MIND

1. God
   a. Praise ye the _____, Praise ye the _____ of the Lord; praise him, O ye servants of the Lord" (Psalms 113:1; 135:1).
   b. We are on earth to do his _____ (James 4:15; 1 John 5:3).
   c. All blessings come from _____ (Acts 14:17).
   d. He gives us every good and perfect _____ (James 1:17).
2. Self
   a. We are his children, he gave us life and made us heirs with _____ to live eternally with him, so we have a proper respect for ourselves (James 2:5).
   b. God loves me. He gave his _____ to die in my place (John 3:16).
   c. God is for _____, and with _____ (Romans 8:31).
   d. I can do all things through _____ (Philippians 4:13).
   e. Prove what is the good and acceptable and perfect _____ of God (Romans 12:2).
3. Others
   a. Should we esteem Christians above others? (Romans 12:10).
   b. Should we flatter others unduly? (1 Thessalonians 2:38).
   c. Who do we care for and share with? (Luke 6:38).
   d. Who should strive to be a good example to others? (Luke 6:45; 1 Timothy 4:12).
   e. How should we feel toward one another? (1 John 4:21; Romans 12:14-16).
   f. What should we desire for our enemies? (Romans 12:14-16).

OUR HELP IN TIMES OF NEED

1. "God is our refuge and strength,_____" (Psalm 46:1).
2. "In all thy ways acknowledge him, and he shall _____" (Proverbs 3:6).

3. "A man's heart deviseth his way; but the Lord _____" (Proverbs 16:9).

## THINGS THAT MAKE FOR PEACE

1. "Justified by faith we shall _____" (Romans 5:1).
2. "And the work of righteousness _____" (Isaiah 32:17a).
3. "The fruit of righteousness is sown _____" (James 3:18).

## THINGS THAT PUT AN END TO STRIFE

1. "Let nothing be done through strife or vain glory; But in lowliness of mind _____. Look not every man on his own things, but every man also _____. Let this mind be in you, which was also in Christ Jesus" (Philippians 2:3-5).
2. "I have learned in whatsoever state I find myself _____" (Philippians 4:11).
3. Control of the tongue
   a. How often is a talebearer the same person who ignited the strife in the first place? Is it ever of any real value to her to repeat and repeat the story? Is this like wood being piled on the fire?
   b. "Where no wood is, there _____, so where there is _____" (Proverbs 26:20).
   c. "Love life, see good days, _____, do good, keep peace and pursue it" (1 Peter 3:10,11).
   d. "Whoso _____ keepeth his soul from troubles" (Proverbs 21:23).
   e. "For in many things we offend all. If any man..., the same is a perfect man and able also to _____" (James 3:2).
   f. "How long will the scorners _____?" (Proverbs 1:22).
      (1). Does it do any good to reprove a scorner? "Reprove not a scorner. A scorner _____, neither will he go _____" (Proverbs 9:8; 15:22).
      (2). How, then, can a scorner be dealt with? "Cast out a _____, and contention shall go out. Yea, _____" (Proverbs 22:10).

## BLESSINGS OF THOSE WHO CEASE FROM STRIFE AND LIVE IN PEACE

1. "Blessed are the _____, for they shall be called the _____" (Matthew 5:9).

89

2. "To the counsellors of peace _____" (Proverbs 12:20b).
3. "The light of the righteous _____, and the lamp of the wicked shall be _____" (Proverbs 13:9).
4. "Behold how good and how pleasant it is _____" (Psalms 131:1).
5. "When a man's ways please the Lord, he maketh_____" (Proverbs 16:7).
6. "Mercy and truth are met together. Righteousness and peace __ _____" (Psalm 85:10).
7. "The righteousness of the perfect shall ____" (Proverbs 11:5a).
8. "To the righteous _____" (Proverbs 13:21).
9. "To the carnally minded is death; but to be spiritually minded is _____" (Romans 8:6).
10. "Never have I seen _____ nor their children _____" (Psalms 37:25).
11. "It is an honor for a man to _____" (Proverbs 20:3a).